oddball@large

oddball@large

bill richardson

Douglas & McIntyre
Vancouver/Toronto

Douglas & McIntyre Ltd.
1615 Venables Street
Vancouver, British Columbia V5L 2H1

These pieces originally appeared, some in slightly different form, in the *Georgia
Straight*, *Vancouver Sun*, *Xtra! West*, the *Globe and Mail*, and *Maclean's*.
"Dogwood" was originally published in *Canada Customs* (Brighouse Press, 1988).

Canadian Cataloguing in Publication Data
Richardson, Bill, 1955–
  Oddball@large

  ISBN 1-55054-626-0

  1. Canadian wit and humor (English)* I. Title. II. Title: Oddball at large.
PS8585.I186O32 1998   C818'.5402   C98-910008-1
PR9199.3.R467O32 1998

Editing by Saeko Usukawa
Cover design by Rose Cowles
Text design and typesetting by Val Speidel
Back cover photograph by Chick Rice
Printed and bound in Canada by Best Book Manufacturers
Printed on acid-free paper ∞

The publisher gratefully acknowledges the support of the Canada Council for the
Arts and of the British Columbia Ministry of Tourism, Small Business and Culture.

We acknowledge the financial support of the Government of Canada through the
Book Publishing Industry Development Program for our publishing activities.

For Sue Wagner,

good friend at large

contents

introduction

if I were a more disciplined writer, and engaged—as I have been—in the business of writing columns, I would long ago have made a habit of clipping the daily papers for articles of vital, gristy interest. Political upheavals. Hollywood scandals. Labour negotiations. The long-range effect of changing technologies on our primary resource industries. And so on. What's more, I would have developed a reliable filing system for those quotidian cullings so that I could have fast and easy access to them. Alas, I am not a disciplined columnist, which is why I can't tell you the name of the institution, and I can't tell you the date, and I can't tell you how much was paid by whatever archive, library or university acquired Michel Tremblay's personal papers a few years back. I am quite sure it happened, however, for this is intelligence I seem to possess, and I have no reason to make up such a thing, or to fantasize it; unless, of course, I tacked so minor an informational remnant to my brain on one of those mornings when someone had laced my coffee with LSD and I was in a hallucinogenic haze.

I imagine that I find this episode in Canadian literary history so memorable because whoever was given permission to come along and shovel all of M. Tremblay's notes and receipts out of his drawers and into acid-free file folders, in order that future scholars might have the pleasure of inhaling his authentic scent while deconstructing him, paid through the nose for the privilege. My recollection is that a whack of cash—in the significant six-figure range—changed hands. My reaction was typically self-centred. "Damn!" I thought. "Such good fortune will never be mine, for I have no papers!"

Oh, I have mountains of scrap that are mostly made of paper. A quick excavation reveals such bijoux as a years-ago Christmas card thoughtfully left by the newspaper delivery person; several 3 × 5 slips of paper inscribed with library call numbers, but with no matching titles; a few dry cleaner's tags; some phone bills from the mideighties; several grocery lists, evidently dating from my dissolute phase, as each contains a reminder to buy gin; car rental contracts; and an obituary from an unidentified paper for a person whose name means nothing to me and to whom I surely meant as little. There is much more such dross besides, but nothing that would make an archivist's heart flutter. There is no correspondence with fascinating contemporaries, no napkins across which are scrawled famous signatures, no cigarettes that bear a lipstick's traces, and no journals or diaries to which I have confided my deepest thoughts, my most intimate secrets, or scathing remarks about the actors and politicians and scientists into whose orbit I might have drifted.

Truth be told, I don't give a damn about most of these absences, other than the journals. That I have not kept a diary is one of my few regrets. Like most other literate people, I imagine, I have made a stab at it from time to time; have gone out at a resolution-making time of year and carefully selected just the right notebook and just the right pen and made an effort—for one week, for two—to sit down each and every evening and record some of the bland events of the day gone by. Always, these record-keeping efforts have petered away, have dwindled. Those aborted diaries now malinger among what passes for my papers, and every now and again I will come across one. Of course, I can never resist the temptation to look within, and it astonishes me how deeply I am pleased by what I find there. It's not that the writing is distinguished, or even good; it's not that I am reminded of my involvement in affairs of state; it's just that those few words are so redolent—even after ten or fifteen years—of a particular place and time and state of mind that details of conversations, of rooms, of trips—details not noted on those sparsely etched pages—resurface after even such gentle prodding. I always feel a pang to think how much more memory I would have access to if only I'd taken the time, the minimal time, to set a few observations down.

These columns are as close as I've come to the discipline of journal keeping. The pieces selected here were not written—with a few exceptions—as a response to news stories, or to events of national importance. They are not civically reactive, and they are not politically analytical. Now and again I have been moved to go on such excursions, but the souvenirs I brought home had a limited shelf life. The columns in this book tend to be small, personal essays that are more inward than outward looking. They were spawned by conversations overheard on public transit; by neighbourhood anomalies (a spate of abandoned shopping carts, the mysterious appearance of speed bumps behind a Buddhist temple); by chance encounters with urban wildlife; by the proclivities of pets; and by the vagaries of close relationships and minor family eruptions. Occasionally, particularly in the pieces that reflect a gay sensibility, you might whiff the smoke of anger. That I write "gay" rather than "queer" says something about who I am generationally, and I was surprised, in rereading this writing, to see how much of it is autumnally coloured. There is a wistful, nostalgic quality—at least, I find there to be—present in the pieces that are preoccupied with the onset of middle age. It can get to be rather much, actually, and at times even I want to slap myself and say, "Oh, get over it!"

These are meanderings in which I say nothing more than what I think and what I feel, and none of it could be said to stray into profundity. Why would anyone care to dally over what are, effectively, my papers? Oh well. It may be some consolation that they are available for a tiny fraction of what was paid for those of M. Tremblay.

I have lamented that this absence of noteworthy personal papers means that they will never be acquired for mighty sums. I should also, I guess, consider the possibility that Tremblay's good fortune will never be mine because he is a major writer with an international reputation, and I have always been on the roster of the little leagues of literature. I don't say this to be self-effacing. It is, after all, where most writers must realistically locate themselves, and it's not a bad place to be. Max Beerbohm said that many "charming talents" are ruined by the urge to make an important statement, and that one must understand whether one's mission in the world is to carry a heavy weight, or whether one's task is more properly to juggle three golden balls in the air. I'd rather the golden balls, although three is a bit much, and I don't think I could lay claim to more than one on most days. But we must make do with what we are given. Morning comes and one picks up one's ball and heads out to play.

I would like to thank the editors who, for reasons they have never made explicit, gave me the chance to bounce my odd ball across their fields and courts. To Cindy Filipenko, Patricia Graham, Max Wyman, Charles Campbell, and Beverley Sinclair—all of whom at different times were generous and understanding of my elastic relationship with deadlines—I owe a particular debt. And as always, I am grateful to Saeko Usukawa and her colleagues at Douglas & McIntyre for their confidence and support.

the randomness of arrivals

Vancouver is a city with much to recommend it. Mountains. Sea. Early daffs. Year-round golf. World-class coffee bars where one doesn't risk being thrown into a psychic tailspin by seeing creative spellings of the word "cappuccino" and which offer minimum-wage employment to youths with interesting eyebrow jewelry. There are condos aplenty, in a wide range of prices. The capricious plate tectonics and the ever-present possibility of an earthquake contribute a certain edge to the dull quotidian. Oh, it's a regular little Eden, where everyone thanks you for not smoking and even the angel posted at the gate has extinguished his burning brand in compliance with city bylaws. However, for all its many virtues, it must be said that Vancouver is also a burg distinguished by an inexplicable paucity of statuary. Such fleshy facsimiles as we have—whether cast in metal or coaxed into being from stone—usually show the sure signs of neglect. No one seems to care for them, which is sad. They must once have meant something to the elders who commissioned them, to the artisans who crafted them, to the citizens who attended their unveilings. But we all know how it goes. Time passes. Familiarity settles in. In short order, public art becomes just another of the unthinking eye's habits: taken in, but not registered. Forgotten directly we pass it by. Save for the war memorial in Victory Square, which has its dependable November 11 spruce-up, most of my city's statuary is left to the tender mercies of the weather and the pigeons and the vandals. No statue is more emblematic of this glum circumstance than that of Christopher Columbus.

That's Cristoforo Colombo, born in Genoa in 1451. That's Cristóbal Colón, who died in Valladolid in 1506. That's our man Chris who, when he wrote, "I made a new voyage to a new heaven and a new earth," was surely not thinking of the corner of North

Grandview and Clark, which is where he has come to sit, all alone and unattended. He has been stuck there since October 11, 1986. That's the date on his plaque, which also reveals that his erection (you should pardon the term) was sponsored by a Genoese consortium, supported by the region of Liguria and the Confratellanza Italo Canadese in memory of the honourable Angelo E. Branca, Q.C.

North Grandview and Clark is at the hub of a light industrial district, just a short hop from where I live. There are a few squat warehouses, a car dealership or two, some cinder-block compounds that house improbable businesses one suspects might be fronts for money-laundering operations, their parking lots strewn every morning with discarded condoms and syringes of dubious sterility. Chris has been stuck in the very dead centre of a temple designed with the aesthetic of the neighbourhood in mind. Ten square and concrete arches surround him on three sides. The base of the statue is an octagonal plinth, from which rises a bollard. This is where Columbus has come to court eternity. Here he perches, rather girlishly, with his stockinged legs crossed decorously in front of the cleat ring. His eyes are downcast, not so much because of diffidence, humility, or shyness as out of an aversion to the imposed environment, which is bland beyond telling. Were Chris to direct his gaze forward, to the east, he would see not the billowing sails of the *Niña*, the *Pinta*, or the *Santa María*; not the swell of the sea or the graceful arc described by a school of dolphins, but the squat structure that houses Valley Ice Products, purveyors of unnamed gasses to anyone who requires them. The surrounding concrete arches, and the unmanicured shrubbery that passes for landscaping, block his view to the north, the south, and the west. In a way, this is a kindness, for in each of those directions is something that is emblematic of travel. Like Oscar Wilde's Happy Prince, his hard cast heart would probably crack with longing if he took in the activities at Martino's Swedish Auto Centre, an enterprise the name of which suggests not only the possibility of wandering but also the same spirit of internationalism that made the king and queen of Portugal hire an Italian mariner to carve out a route to the spicy Indies. How could he bear to stare out to the west, onto the chugging and shunting that enlivens the railway tracks, or to the south where the SkyTrain—Vancouver's automated light rapid transit system—whooshes by every couple of minutes, and where Jesse's Moving and Storage has erected a huge sign emblazoned with the taunting question, "MOVING?". Taunting because that is one thing Christopher Columbus is not doing now. Oh, no. He's not going anywhere.

Gravel, weeds, shards of pop and beer bottles, cigarette butts, bits of foil: all the usual litter is scattered around. It's not a place for a young man to spend his time, and this Columbus is very young indeed. He can't be more than 12 or 13. Look at his fresh face, his curly hair, his boyish cap. He is years away from going to sea, years and years away from sailing into a Cuban bay and reporting that "the days are warm and the nights balmy, like May in Spain, in Andalusia." It will be two decades at least before he explores villages and finds "dogs which never barked, and wild birds living tame in the houses, and wonderfully crafted fishing nets"; before he reports back to his royal sponsors that "the loveliness of this country . . . is so marvellous. It surpasses all others in amenity and beauty as daylight exceeds night." How could this boy ever imagine that one day he would kidnap some of the very people who came out to him in friendship, who showed every kindness to a pasty-skinned voyager? He could never anticipate the way they would keep on trying, unreasonably, to escape when he wanted to take them back as some kind of proof. And surely the last thing on his mind would be the possibility that he might end up in such a God-forsaken part of the world as the corner of North Grandview and Clark. But there he is, for all to see.

Not many care to come, mind you. Chris is not much visited. There is a drinking fountain adjacent to the statue that attracts some cyclists and the occasional thirsty passerby. It is a fine fountain, blessed with commendable pressure. The jet has an impressive trajectory. Once—I remember it was a Sunday, last summer—a skinny young man stopped there to take a drink. He was wearing baggy skateboarding pants. He carried his T-shirt, and his upper body was dense with tattoos. He drank for a long time, then splashed water on his face, on his colourful chest. He cupped one hand. He filled it with water. He turned towards Columbus, who might have been watching out of the corner of an eye, then tilted back his head and baptized himself. He shook himself, grinned, and sauntered off on his heron legs, laughing. He sauntered off and left Columbus high and dry, not a thought in his hot, bronze brain, not so much as a glimmer of a dream of how he would set sail from Palos on August 3, 1492, and finish up here, alone on his bollard, leaning forward ever so slightly, poised to slip right off the edge of the world, never suspecting how far he would fall, never dreaming of how he would come to so sorry an end.

vacation diary of an inveterate eavesdropper

New York City, Penn Station waiting room.
Woman, fifty-ish, speaking to man with cane.

So I say to her, Can I borrow your beads? She looks at me like she doesn't know what I'm talking about. Your beads, I say, those yellow beads. The ones you wear all the time. The yellow ones. She says, Yellow beads? You mean that antique piece? I say, Antique, antique, what antique, how should I know how old they are? She says, You mean the antique piece I wore to Martin's party? I wasn't at Martin's party, I say, I'm talking about the yellow beads! Oh, she says, the yellow beads! Oh, those. Oh, I thought you meant the antique piece I wore to Martin's party! No, I say, I only met Martin once, why should he invite me to his party? I was talking about the yellow beads. Oh, the yellow beads, she says. Sure, you can borrow those. But I couldn't let you borrow the other. Not the antique piece. I couldn't let it out of my sight. It's just too old and valuable. And I say, That's fine, because it's the yellow beads I wanted to borrow. So she gets them for me. But I was mad! Oh, I was some mad! Where does she get off talking to me like that? Huh? I mean, after I made her barbecue that time even though my kids were sick and you remember how she said to me after that how there was nothing in the world she wouldn't do for me? Nothing? You remember? So why give me all that guff about those yellow beads, huh? I mean, who's she gonna leave them to when she dies? Arthur's girlfriend?

*New York City, lobby of the Plymouth Theater during the
intermission for Edward Albee's* A Delicate Balance.
Bearded man, mid-thirties, talking to his date.

I met Albee at a party last fall. I gave him my theory about this play. I told him that I thought it was all about adoption and abandonment. It's perfectly plain. And he said, No, that wasn't what it was about at all, and I told him that I just couldn't agree with him. He said, Well, I wrote it, after all, aren't I entitled some input? I told him I took his point, but that I thought my ideas were perhaps even more valid. I think he was quite taken with that. He told me he was fascinated and that he'd invite me up to his place in Montauk sometime this summer. Yes, he said I could come for the weekend, and we could continue the discussion. No, I haven't heard from him yet. I expect he'll call soon.

Joffrey, New Hampshire, restaurant. Family of three.

Mother: It's called swordfish, honey. Won't you try some? It's grilled!
Child: No!
Father: But John Henry, you see how much Mommy and I are enjoying it!
Together: Mmmmmmmm! Good!
Child: No! No! I wanna have Froot Loops!
Mother: (Sighs)
Father: (Sighs)
Mother: Well then, I guess if that's the case, there's only one thing we can do.
Father: That's right. I guess we'll have to take you back to the little boy store where we got you. We'll just have to return you.
Mother: That's right. We'll take you back and we'll get another little boy and bring him home.
Child: Wh- wh- what?
Mother: Oh, but we'll keep your toys.
Father: Yes, the new little boy will need something to play with.
Mother: Like your videos, and your horse, and your cars.
(Long silence, punctuated by the chewing of fish and low snuffling.)
Child: You mean—you mean—you don't love me?

Mother: Oh, John Henry!
Father: Of course we love you, son. We love you very much!
Mother: Where would you get the idea that we don't love you? Try some swordfish?
Child: Froot Loops! I want Froot Loops!

*New York City, sidewalk cafe, West Village. Young blonde woman,
dressed in black, talking to her male companion.*

No, you tell me, Tyrone. Why, why, why, should I be with this man? I mean, why should I feel obliged to be going out with him and his wretched parents tonight? To a play? Why? I mean, like, why? I know, Tyrone. I mean, I haven't forgotten that I married him, but what does that mean? I mean, what does it really, really mean? I mean, if I'm going to be with someone, I want to be with someone who feeds me, who nourishes me, someone who enriches me! Know what I mean? I mean, I want to be with someone who knows what we're looking at when we go to an antique store, someone who has something to say about the art on the wall in a gallery, someone who when we go to the symphony has something to say other than "that's nice." I mean, I feel like I can't breathe half the time. I really can't breathe. And I have to be able to breathe if I'm going to act. And I am going to act, Tyrone. I mean, no one and nothing will stop me from doing that. Because I am an artist. Because I must, I must, I must practise my craft!

*New York City, West 43rd Street, near Broadway.
Older couple who have just been panhandled.*

She: What did he say?
He: He said he was collecting for the United Negro Pizza Fund.
She: I've never heard of that.
He: Me neither.
She: What did you give him?
He: A quarter.
She: That's nice.

mr. grasshead is dead

There's this woman on the Sky-Train. She's talking to her friend, another woman. This other woman, I mean the friend, she's in a lousy way. She's crying. She dabs at her eyes with a Kleenex. Something bad is going down. It is a tender moment, really tender. I look away to give them their privacy. I know when not to intrude, discretion being my middle name and all. But when I turn my head, you know, like out of courtesy, doesn't it just happen that my left ear is perfectly placed to pick up their conversation! What a pickle! Especially since my left ear is the keen one and all. The woman, that's the first woman, she says to the other woman, that's her friend, the one who's crying, she says, "I know just what you're going through. I bawled for a week after I had Charlie put down. They're just animals but you get so attached to them."

They could have been talking about husbands or they could have been talking about cats. I don't know. I'm no eavesdropper after all and anyway they were getting off at the next stop and I really couldn't imagine trailing them, especially since I myself had just about been shoved over the cliff of tears by all their sadness. I'm that way, you know. I'm a regular sponge for emotion, too sensitive to live, really, and all that weeping was just so reminiscent of my own recent sadness. My eyes were all moist, but in my dry mind's eye I saw an all-too-vivid picture of my dear Mr. Grasshead. Mr. Grasshead, whom I loved. Mr. Grasshead, who is dead. Oh! Oh! Oh, Mr. Grasshead! I miss you so!

This is the way with the past, don't you find? It hammers its stake into the individual psyche as ruthlessly as Judith drove her peg into the heart of Holofernes. Blow, blow, you lusty winds of the here and now! Blow as you will, with all your might! You will never dislodge the sturdy pup tent that shelters the memory of days gone by! Mr. Grasshead taught me that. Yes. Yes. It was Mr. Grasshead who brought me face to face once again with my own forgotten story. With my prairie boyhood, those long-ago days spent among the rows of waving wheat and the undulating flax and the genuflecting rape, which is an unfortunate name for a grain if ever there was one. I could have stayed, maybe should have stayed, but I longed for distant places. The siren song of the city rang in my ears. I became—so I thought—impervious to the magnetism of primary production. I forsook the photosynthetic charms of easy agrarian proximity in favour of concrete. I had forgotten it all until I was given the little bag of dirt and seed that became Mr. Grasshead.

It was my birthday. August 11. It comes round sooner than you think, and just in case you care to know, I'm registered at Birks, where they have many fine items well suited to some of my extraordinary sensitivity and all. It was my birthday, like I said, and like I do every year I had assembled everyone I knew with enough moolah and chutzpah to get themselves down to Birks and pick me up something really nice, or at least interesting. Coming as he did after all those champagne glasses and martini shakers and monogrammed sterling napkin rings, Mr. Grasshead was a bit of a shock, I can tell you. A disappointment, even. "Thanks," I managed to choke out to whatever clod deigned to give me this schmutz-filled, dun-coloured muslin sack with its stick-on eyes and elastic-wrapped nose. The directions were simple. Water it. Grass would grow, like hair. "Fat fuckin' chance," I thought to myself, in an uncharacteristically insensitive moment, and hurled the thing into a corner. It wasn't love at first sight, that's for dang sure!

But the next day, he caught my eye. Poor Mr. Grasshead, lying all forlorn beside something exquisite by Baccarat. Something about the sight of him touched my heart. "Oh, all right," I said. And I set him in a dish (Limoges) and watered him as per the instructions. I didn't hold out much hope, since I have had bad luck with things horticultural, ever since I dug up my own roots and tumbled out to the coast. But within a couple of days, he was showing some green stubble. Within two weeks, he had a full head of lovely green hair. When had I last successfully grown anything? I couldn't recall at all. By month end, I was smitten. He was every inch himself. He was Mr. Grasshead, living up to his name, a swatch of prairie right there on top of the stereo speaker. And oh, but he was a cheery little soul, with his button-bright eyes and his painted-on smile and his verdant, wavy do. Oh, tiny tuft of turf! Oh, merry wee sod! He was my buddy. He was just the kind of friend I like, what with his minimal requirements and all. No 4:00 a.m. phone calls, no beseeching pleas for long-term loans, no anguished conversations about love gone wrong. Just throw some water at him now and again and he returned your scant attentions a hundredfold. Unconditional love, that was what Mr. Grasshead offered. Demands? He didn't know the meaning of the word. All that winter he lived happily in his dish. I would stick my nose into his scalp and the smell of his brain working would yank me back to who I was, from whence I came. It was healing. It was rich. Oh, Mr. Grasshead! Cheaper than the therapist and twice as attractive! Where are you now?

I had to go away. I had to travel. I left instructions for his care. Something happened. I'm not one to assign blame. Maybe it was the cleaners. He was set atop the baseboard heater. Down there, out of sight. Out of mind. January went by. February went by. The chill months. Hear what I'm saying? I don't doubt that he sent out parched calls of alarm. But I didn't hear them, for all my exquisite sensitivity. And when I came home, I found him. Late, much too late. I set him outside, hoping for a miracle, hoping to revive him in the rains of March. The neighbour's dog saw him, mistook him for a tennis ball. Hear what I'm saying? Mr. Grasshead. He dead, man. He dead. I remember him every time I take a madeleine from the Limoges plate that was once his home.

Pray with me. Dear Lord, as we enter this season of resurrection, think on your servant Mr. Grasshead and remember his name. Scatter his seed on fertile ground that the wind may once again know the caress of his blades. Say hi to him for me, Lord. He was Mr. Grasshead. I loved him. My good dead friend.

another tuesday morning

Yes, well, here we go again, it's yet another Tuesday (could be Wednesday, could be Thursday), it's 7:30 a.m. and you're in the Broadway SkyTrain station, standing decorously back from the yellow line, standing well back as you are mindful of the dreadful consequences of slippage, standing well back as you are after all Canadian and pacific (though not passive) by nature and you don't want to inconvenience or unsettle anyone by taking a tumble, by delivering your flesh to the track and the wheels, don't want anyone to be late for work, don't want to inconvenience your executor with the dry-cleaning bills that might come his way what with the untoward spray of fluids such clumsiness would certainly precipitate, to say nothing of the coffee that might slosh out of some rider's carry-out cup onto rayon or silk if the train shuddered at all on impact or came to a screeching halt, and you stand back because you don't want to cause a rush-hour disruption, don't want to endure the indignity of being called a "medical emergency" on some dumbass radio traffic report, and the trains are coming in and heading out, slouching toward Waterfront, it's all they have on their minds, they are drawn there against their will, they couldn't stop themselves if they wanted to, it's destiny, nothing more, nothing less, it's built in, those trains, they can't wait to get to the end of the line where they will spawn, recreate themselves in their own image, turn around and head on out to Scott Road for more of the same.

Oh yes, it's Tuesday, it's 7:30 a.m., and yet another train pulls up, this is the third or fourth you've watched glide into the crowded station, you've been waiting, vainly hoping not for a seat or anything so extravagant, just for a car that looks as though it will contain enough oxygen to sustain you as far as Stadium, surely that shouldn't be too much to ask for, but yes, evidently it is, and finally you can't avoid it any longer, and when your chosen conveyance has disgorged a few dishevelled automatons you let the forward thrust of the throng carry you in, you find a square foot of floor, plant your feet at hips' width and the jostle subsides and the doors shut and now it's too late and you can't move at all, this must be what it's like to be a cherry tomato on a fat man's plate at an all-you-can-eat buffet, everything slopping around, mismatched, running together, oozing, you are paralytic, and what's more you are staring directly down the left ear canal of a man with an attractive profile and a very dirty collar.

You can't do otherwise, you are inches away, staring down his ear canal, more properly the auditory canal, you think, as words from a sixth-grade project insinuate themselves into the upper reaches of your memory—cochlea, tympanum, hammer, anvil, stirrup—and you are pleased to note that his ear is clean, that's good, that speaks well of his character, that mitigates somewhat the grubbiness of the collar, and you remember that you yourself have once again forgotten to buy Q-Tips, and you would surreptitiously check the state of your own ears if only you could move your arm but you're wedged in so tight you think you'll need to smear yourself with K-Y just to get out of there and you see that there is a tiny nick on the delicately whorled inside of his earlap and you wonder if he removes those wiry hairs by whacking them back with a straight razor as you have done from time to time, and dangling from the lobe is an earring, a thin hoop with a discreet little cross, perhaps he is a Christian, perhaps God whispers to him in that very ear, and it occurs to you that you could whisper to him as well, you could whisper "I love you," which for a split second you believe you do and what could he do about it anyway, he couldn't run, he couldn't hit you, who knows, he might even mistake you for the voice of God, oh go on, you might as well say it, and just as you're about to act on this impulse you feel a fleshy pressure from your starboard side. It is a hand rubbing against your own.

You turn your head—you have that much mobility—to see what's up, it's another man, his hair hangs over his ears, but his collar is visible, it's clean, starched even, and then the train pulls into Main Street and a few people get off and you adjust your position ever so slightly and about twenty more people pile in and you're stuck tighter than ever before and now you find yourself with the second man's attaché case stuck between your legs, it's rubbing against your perineum, your bulbocavernosus and pubococcygeal muscles contract and dilate, and still his hand is touching your hand, you can't pull it away, there is no place to pull it, and he pretends he is oblivious, he stares at an ad that advises him to buy Lipsorex whenever he feels an incipient cold sore start to tingle and you look back into the ear canal of the man to whom you almost gave yourself, whatever did you see in him anyway, he is infuriating, you want to whisper "You asshole, don't you care, after all we've been to each other, stand up for yourself, claim me," and you look down and realize that he too carries a briefcase and what's more he's using it to make a navel assault on the man with the clean collar whose important papers and agenda are in such close proximity to your own balls, oh it is sordid, sordid, one is faithless, the other promiscuous, men, men, they are all alike, and then you are at Stadium and then you are out on the platform, and then they are gone and they have forgotten you before the train is out of sight and you know they are happy together, well, they deserve each other and you say fuck you, fuck you, and oh, oh, oh, how you miss them, yes, yes, you miss them already.

an odd wednesday morning

As near as I can figure it—and I could very easily be mistaken about this, having erred once or twice over the course of my already long life—there are three possibilities. One is that the world is odd all the time, but that our preoccupation with the dull round of the everyday obscures conspicuous weirdness from view. Two is that there does in fact exist a kind of median degree of oddness, a daily ration to which we grow accustomed over time, but that every so often the planets align themselves in such a way that this quota is exceeded and because of the consequent unnatural coalescence of curious occurrences the world takes on an especially loony aspect. Three is that we possess internal sensors that alert us to the presence of oddness around us, and that a biorhythmic cycle outside our conscious control sometimes brushes this internal radar with preternatural acuity. I ruminate now on so speculative a cud because I am setting this down at the end of a day that has left me fairly gobstruck with wave after wave of oddness; the kind of day that makes you feel as if the Creator has gone to Reno on the fun bus, and left Fellini in charge of seeing that things unfold as they should.

Oddness reigned from the word go. I was awakened by the cat singing her early-morning hymn to the hairball goddess, a wheezing racket like the throat-wracked gunning of a recalcitrant Harley in the hallway. The offending particles, when they were expunged and removed from the carpet, left behind a stain that looked remarkably like the map of France, a pattern that was repeated in the cloud cover when I stepped outside. On my way to work, I passed three separate early-morning panhandlers, two of whom were singing "Clementine," and one of whom was playing it on the mouth organ. As if that were not enough, my path intersected, on three different streets, with three apparently unrelated individuals carrying three apparently unrelated mattresses on their backs, each one oblivious to the considerable wind that was blowing about them, each one heading north. I checked the paper for word of a convention, meeting, or other reunion that might explain such a sight. There was none. Over lunch hour, in order to maintain some semblance of solvency, I had to do minor transactions at two separate banks. In a touch that I can only call Cronenbergian, the male tellers I dealt with in these two establishments were dead ringers one for the other. En route back to the office, a gorgeous double rainbow heaved itself out of Coal Harbour and described an arc that would suggest the presence of a pot of gold somewhere in the rough vicinity of Ballantyne Pier. As I studied it, wondering if it had anything to do with the eventual destination of the mattress carriers, a woman detached herself from the crowd and handed me a red plaid bag. "Here," she said, "I have two," and walked away, leaving me holding a perfectly lovely travel iron. I'll be needing such a thing if I wind up going to France, as both the clouds and the cat vomit would seem to presage.

I am not making any of this up. It was scarcely noon, and I felt that I was about to slip into some interdimensional realm from which I might never emerge without the help of the *X-Files*. I went for a walk to clear my head. My perambulations took me down a west-end street. I was looking fondly at the high rises, trying to remember under which of the roofs I'd sheltered for intimate moments, and with whom, when my attention was caught by a tremendously raucous carry-on from above. Four and twenty black birds, at the very least, had arranged themselves into a negritic aureole in the stripped and uppermost twigs of a chestnut tree. What a to-do, as if a convicted sex offender had been released to a halfway branch in their neighbourhood.

I am not keen of eye, and it took me a moment to spot the object of their harsh derision. It was an owl, dirty white and blinking. She sat calmly in one of the tree's convenient V's, a tuft of something mouse-like in her talons, twisting her neck in that show-off double-jointed way owls have, utterly unconcerned at the brouhaha erupting all around her, everything about her posture and stance broadcasting, "Oh, fuck off," but in the nicest possible way. My, how odd! A midday owl in the middle of the city, a successful urban hunter, the very spirit and embodiment of calm and achieved purpose, and the killing but ineffectual clamour of a murder of crows, and then the owl simply lifting off, hardly even moving her wings, like the holy spirit moving over the waters, and the crows parting to make a voluble corridor, and then, in the time it takes an owl to blink her eyes, or so it seemed, she was gone, gone, gone, and the earth might have paused in its spinning for just the merest fraction of a second, and a deep, pure silence sang before the crows erupted again, and the planet got back to the business of grinding out the dying year, pulling oddness after oddness from out its gaudy, wonderful sleeves.

a thursday evening stroll

Seven to one. Isn't that the ratio we trot out when we stack up dog and human years, one against the other? Like most comparisons, this one is invidious. It's also meaningless, a telling example of how we try to make sense of other species by qualifying them and quantifying them and measuring them against ourselves. Why can't we accord dogs the simple courtesy of acknowledging that they lead lives that are wholly distinct and separate from our own? Other than demonstrating conversancy with the seven times tables, you gain nothing from telling a five-year-old pooch, "If you were human, you'd be 35!"

Having said this, I have to own how I felt a special kinship with my dog when, as recently happened, her own chronological accumulation pulled up alongside mine, and then—according to the famous formula—forged on ahead. "Oh Smoke," I would whisper to her in those tender moments a man shares with his pup on the couch, "this is a time that will come no more! Never again will we share the same age! We're equals, honey! Equals!"

She would raise her head from my lap, roll her indifferent sloe eyes and quietly belch. The fumes from her lamb-and-rice designer kibble coagulated into a fusty balloon above her head. Were I a cartoonist I would have inscribed it with these words: "Equals, hell! The day I pick up your poop in a plastic bag, fella, you can call us equals!"

The French have an expression of which I am fond, and which I sometimes articulate on occasions that call for a certain savoir-faire. It is *entre loup et chien*—between the wolf and the dog. Some insightful Gallic imagist coined it to describe twilight.

By nature, I am an indoors person. Left to my own devices, I would spend my evenings under cover, reading, talking on the phone and watching *Golden Girls* reruns. But Smoke requires that we go out and promenade along the boulevard, just as the lupine night is showing its jaws to the canine day. Thanks to her I have very often seen, as I wouldn't have otherwise, how the blue bruise of crepuscular sky deepens to purple, to black. Thanks to Smoke, I know twilight: that weird, suspended parenthetical time when normalcy is not the norm and odd moments happen.

Is it the quality of light, the weight of myth, or simply an accumulation of expectation that imparts a mystical, magical quality to twilight occurrences?

Last night we passed two weathered drunks on a bench. That's common enough in our neighbourhood. But it's not so usual for one to be teaching the other to use his fingers to produce a good, loud whistle; an absorbing project that had displaced their paper-bag shrouded bottles as the focus of their attention. That's the stuff of twilight, not of noon.

A block further on, we found half a fortune cookie, its pink prognosticatory slip still protruding. "You have nothing to fear," it said, which is a comforting thought as night comes on.

We heard a lullaby coming from one apartment window, and the interesting sounds of lovemaking spilling from another nearby; an arresting, even cautionary juxtaposition. We heard two women talking about a car purchase. "What did you buy?" asked one. "A Toyota," her friend answered.

In the aftermath of that ordinary twilight exchange, two things happened. At the moment I remembered that "a Toyota" is a perfect palindrome, I looked up and saw two huge herons describe an arc in the wolf-and-dog sky above us. I imagined that the beat of their wings left tracks in the air, a trail that resembled a big double helix. It was a small but potent coincidence of events, a strange and heightened moment that engendered the full-form birth of an apt and impressive palindrome, right there on the spot. I hurried home to write it down, and was delighted to see that it took the form of a poem that resembled the herons' flight path.

Dog and wolf, on time,
are timid?
Ha!
Ah,
dim it, era!
Emit no flow: DNA, God.

So pleased was I with my insight and cleverness that I hurried to show the poem to my partner, who said, "It doesn't make sense. Besides, a man of your years should have something better to do with his time."

Sense? Since when did mysticism have to make sense? My years? I thought to mention that, were I a dog, I'd only be 5½. But what was the point. Smoke was on the couch. The wolf was at the door. The prophet was without honour. All was as it should be.

It was time for bed. The last thing I saw, as I drifted off, was the clock's digital report. 12:53. Seven to one.

obéissance de chien

As for me, I am doing everything I can, linguistically and culturally, to keep this shaky federation we call Canada together. Perhaps this is vain quixotic tilting. I see how the deck is stacked. I know full well that I'm but one little man, swimming against the riptide in a sea of discontent. It would be easy, and perhaps even prudent, for us to give it all up, abandon ship, retire to our corners, and suck our separate oranges. But I feel honour bound to try and try and try again, until the sponge of hope is wrung well and truly dry. I feel honour bound to take my abstract longing for unity and bring it to bear on day-to-day situations. Only by rendering the theoretical concrete can we survive.

For example: I am addicted to bank machines. Five or six times a day, I belly up to a wall of cash, and coax it to spit greenbacks. Each and every time, I select the French-language option. While the distant computer is doing its complex figuring, I engage the screen in a little dialogue.

«*Insérez votre carte.*»

«*D'accord,*» I say, pursing my lips and rolling my r's with Gallic relish.

«*Composez votre numéro personnel.*»

«*Avec plaisir,*» I answer, brandishing my index finger with devil-may-care bravado, and massaging the numbers that are my "open sesame" to a cave chockablock with crisp 20s. I select from either "*chèques*" or "*épargnes.*"

«*Attendez s.v.p.*»

While I wait, I chant a soothing litany. «*Ah, oui. Bien sûr. Pas de problème. Prenez votre temps. Monsieur Thibaud va à l'épicerie. Son et lumière. Savoir-faire. Fêves au lard. Voulez-vous prendre un café?*»

And then, when I've retrieved "*la monnaie,*" as well as "*ma carte,*" and when the machine has bid me a fond and altogether unnecessary "*bonne journée,*" I make my way home. Sometimes, I stop en route for some artery-clogging "*poutine.*"

I appreciate that these exertions on my part, while personally satisfying, have little effect on our society as a whole. I know that I have to reach out beyond myself.

And so, in order that I might broaden my range of influence, I decided to enrol my dog, Smoke, in an immersion obedience school.

Anyone who has felt similarly moved will hasten to tell you this is not a chore that should be lightly undertaken. It requires enormous commitment, right from the day of registration—a procedure I have just endured.

As immersion obedience schools are few and far between, and as available places are doled out on a first come, first serve basis, pet owners who wish their animals to have the advantages of bilingual training must often camp out on the sidewalk the night before signing up, much as they might for, say, a Stones concert.

The atmosphere in our queue was jovial, optimistic, and now and then, ever so slightly competitive. Here is a random culling of remarks I overheard.

"Even if Quebec separates, I still think it will be useful if Brandy can respond to *assieds-toi* as readily as to sit. After all, someday she might want to travel."

"My husband wants Pepe in Japanese immersion. 'Pacific Rim,' he says. 'Pacific Rim!' He's like a bloody broken record. Well, I just finally put my foot down. 'Listen, buster,' I said, 'it's still Canada, and any decent dachshund can *couche* as well as he can lie down. So he's going into French! Sayonara!' And I stomped right down here!"

"My parrot is already fluent. When she says, '*Polly voudrait bien un biscuit,*' you'd think she was from Trois Rivières! And you should hear her sing *Alouette*!"

"I understand that immersion dogs score appreciably higher on retrieval tests."

And so on. The night brightened. Dawn came. By 10:00 a.m., my forbearance had borne fruit. On Tuesday Smoke begins. «*Oh, Fumée! Quelle chance!*» I burbled once I got home. She looked up from her bed, rolled her eyes and sneezed. «*Fou! Fou! Fou!*»

My Lord, but I was pleased. She's a natural! Three days shy of starting school and she's already showing signs of becoming a keen political analyst. There's hope yet, my friends. *Ne pas se jeter par la fenêtre! Nous avons encore de l'espoir.*

a shaggy horse story

Lhe English language, for all its magnificence, is freighted with lacunae, particularly when it comes to describing emotions. As near as I know, we don't have a word or phrase to identify the dull ache that wells up when a favourite watering hole—where many an evening has been wasted courting sweet oblivion—closes its doors. The French call such a longing after grubbiness *nostalgie de la boue*. I felt a moist wash of this *nostalgie* the other day when I saw that the Shaggy Horse had been put out to pasture.

The Shaggy was for many years a Vancouver gay bar, and once upon a long time ago it was a regular haunt of mine. I started going there when I was in my early twenties, at a time in the bar's attenuated and changing life when it was popular mostly with a mature crowd—that is, men who are about the age I am now. I think I enjoyed being the youngest person in the room—a pleasure I ages ago forsook—and I also got a kick out of the decor. The interior design had obviously been concocted to live up to the club's name. There was a big neon horse rearing up in one corner, and the walls were hung with what looked to be a virulently hirsute brand of shag carpet. Now, it might have been something else, like that ferny spray-on insulation you sometimes see bearding the roofs of car parks. It wasn't the kind of stuff you'd actually want to touch, just for the sake of putting a name to it. It was a colour not found in nature—which is hardly surprising, when you consider that it had been permeated by the smoke of thousands of cigarettes—and the overall effect was rather like being on the inside of a rank vacuum bag. I loved it. For a while, I went almost every weekend. It was a refuge, a place to hang out, a place to drink, a place where the atmosphere was heavy with the possibility of sex. I don't mind telling you that getting lucky was an item on my agenda. It didn't happen very often. Timid, retiring, skinny, and bespectacled, I was a dud as a sexual outlaw. Even so, it is a truth universally acknowledged that anyone who willingly and frequently courts the combination of too much beer and two in the morning is bound to get some action, and I guess I saw my share.

I knew the names of a few of the Shaggy regulars, and had a nodding acquaintance with some of the others. Many of the alumnae are still in the city, though of course a disproportionate number have died. Over the last 10 years we've all grown accustomed, if not inured, to watching the sad and familiar wasting, sometimes gradual, sometimes swift, whittle away at the flesh and spirit of one-time drinking buddies. Sometimes it's harder to take than others. Sometimes I'll see a guy across the street, and note how he has dwindled, and remember that we once went skin to skin, almost 20 years ago, when we'd been lulled into believing that sex was no more consequential than a handshake, and no one worried about the repercussions, or was mindful of the irony, of getting lucky.

To lay claim to luck is a vanity. It suggests that others who have been dealt a different, and seemingly lesser, hand are somehow worse off. That is a blinkered way of seeing the world. Having said that, though, the truth is that I do feel, in this regard at least, lucky: lucky to be here, and fatter now than I was then. The truth is that when I look back over those many years to where I was and all I did, and when I pass by the late and lamented Shaggy Horse, I think of how continuance in the world relies on nothing much more than being in the right place when the near misses come along. I think I know how the circus knife-thrower's lovely assistant feels when the last of his dozen daggers whistles past and thunks into the wall, half an inch above her head.

doomed proposals: 1

I try to be a good existentialist, living for the moment, with nary a regret for all that is past and giving not a tinker's damn for what lies ahead. Even so, I fret about the bleak future of the Canada Pension Plan. Day after day we hear grim bleatings from one quarter or another. Every newscast and broadsheet assaults us with the prophecies of doom-spouting Cassandras. They warn that within a very few years the well will be dry, the oasis will be parched, the trough will be empty, and *then* we baby boomers will get our comeuppance for all those years of hogging the best jobs while foisting our tastes and sensibilities and our awful nostalgia on subsequent generations.

Try as I might not to let these dim prospects strip the lustre from the pearly necklace of my middle age, I'm feeling unsettled. Irrational, even. I'm starting to act out in inappropriate ways and places. Common civility is imperilled. Just the other day—when I happened to be lunching at Denny's—I upbraided some senior citizens who were chowing down with an improvidence that belied their years and that I found impertinent beyond bearing. I couldn't stop myself from imagining the enormity of their bill, and it made me see red. "Hey, Pops," I called, rather shrilly, "hold on a second! Couldn't you and the missus *share* a piece of banana cream pie, rather than having individual slices? Geez! Go easy on your expenditures, old man, or there won't be any money left for me!" I must say the phrase "Fuck off, junior" is very unbecoming when it comes from a near octogenarian.

Where are we to look for news to mitigate these bleak economic prospects? Well! I, for one, was considerably heartened by the reports coming out of the recent World Conference on Auto Urine

Therapy in Panjim, India (*cf. The Globe and Mail*, February 27, 1996). Delegates to that confab, organized by the Water of Life Foundation, insist that regular imbibing of one's own pee is a tonic like no other. It's been going on for 5000 years, and even such vaunted personages as Sarah Miles swear by it. What glad tidings are these! *Quelle joie, alors!* For even if our social security system fails us utterly, the various hormones, enzymes, vitamins, and minerals that we thoughtlessly flush away day in and day out can evidently sustain us into our old age. When we're trying to make our pension cheques stretch to cover cat food and Ritz crackers, we will be able to take comfort in knowing that there's a pot of gold in every bladder! Why, we'll always be able to get by! The phrase "piss poor" has been proven oxymoronic.

At present, urine drinking is practised widely in the West only by those who have been cast adrift at sea on life rafts and have mislaid their desalination pills. As well, certain frat boys and members of some of our more elite military agencies have been known to encourage one another to knock back a pint of recycled water in the spirit of good fun. By and large, however, the suggestion that one might smilingly quaff down a steaming glass of even so enzyme-rich a pick-me-up—bottled at the source, no less—will receive little more than muted enthusiasm from most beverage lovers.

What this means, of course, is that there is work to be done! Those who are entrepreneurial of spirit will now have the chance to make hay while the sun shines! The multifaceted urine industry is about to take off, and take off big! All the societal signs and economic indicators are right. So, if you want to get in on the ground floor, if you want to be Number One (no pun intended!), there are numbers of fertile fields you might consider sowing.

For instance, some insightful soul will surely want to develop a workshop to help potential urine swillers overcome their groundless fear of chugging the stuff back. It could be you! Develop a reassuring curriculum, pointing out the long and honourable history of auto-urine therapy. Tell your students about how pee-sluicing pioneer J. W. Armstrong cured himself of tuberculosis in six weeks by availing himself of his private wet bar. Stress that former Indian Prime Minister Morarji Desai drank a glass of his own urine every day, and lived to be 99. There's no need to point out that the day he passed on, so to speak, was the day he discovered that his midafternoon refresher was not, in fact, lemonade. And what about the possibilities of Urine Bars? Human beings are social creatures, and no one likes to drink alone. Since the bar concept has gone gangbusters for booze and juice and coffee, why not capitalize both on the by-product of those great diuretic agents and on Everyman's need for social intercourse? There's plenty of latitude for creativity here, especially when it comes to questions of design. Why not devise an enchanting soundscape featuring, say, the sound of running water? And let's not forget about urinary accessories! All fashionable pee drinkers will want T-shirts emblazoned with evangelistic messages ("Piss Off! I Do!"), bumper stickers ("I Brake for Urine Bars!"), purpose-built mugs, or—for practical folk who want to forgo the intermediary stage of a cumbersome vessel—colourful tubing to connect orifice directly to orifice! Why not? We are only limited by our imaginations! And this is just the beginning.

You see how it is? Just when you thought there was no point in going on, I've come along to enliven your days. There is no need to thank me. None whatsoever. I'm doing the work God made me for. I'm answering my call. I'm fulfilling my mission. And it's always a pleasure to serve you.

blessed among men

a few days shy of Christmas, I dreamed I had a baby. Gave birth to one, I mean. As dreams go, it was very arresting. I was not alarmed, but I was sure surprised: surprised that this was happening at all, especially to me. It was the last thing I'd have expected. It was nothing I'd ever asked or hoped for. Also, I was surprised—and rather pleased—that it came to me so easily, this birthing business. My baby didn't have to fight its way out of any of the available holes or crevices, and there was no pushing or panting or straining on my part. I simply felt a stirring, looked down, and there it was: this welling foetus, growing out of the region of my navel, rising up like bread from a pan. The most benign of tumours. A ripening peach. Just at the moment it was about to detach itself—at which point I had the impression it would float up and bounce along the ceiling—I came to. I lay there in bed, inhabited by a slight throbbing in my thighs, as well as by a peculiar feeling of absence, and by the lingering suspicion that herein lay a message, a sign or portent to which I should pay attention. After all, miracles of an obstetric variety are known to occur at this time of year. If only I had remained somnolent for just another minute or two, I might have heard an annunciatory voice pronounce me—possibly in Latin—blessed among men. All day long I pondered these things in my heart. On the way home from work, I stopped at the drugstore to pick up a pregnancy test.

Whenever I browse the shelves of the local London Drugs, I get a bad case of vulva envy. Gals are so lucky! All us fellas have access to is shaving supplies and a few varieties of condoms. But gals! Gals can choose from all those pads and panty liners and sprays and gels and deodorants and creams. There's row after row of something for every vaginal microclimate. So, I wasn't so very surprised to find that in this one quite small pharmacy there were no fewer than seven pregnancy tests. I decided to buy them all.

The pharmacist gave me the well-practised supercilious look of someone who is often asked for free methadone samples. "They're all the same, you know," she said, as I set my septet on her counter. "They test for a hormone in the urine, and they're all the same." I gave her a kind of gosh-shucks Jimmy Stewart shrug, in order that she might think me a nervous father-to-be who wanted to leave no stone unturned in uncovering the truth of his happy wife's gravidity. "They're all the same," she said, more firmly, as I pushed them toward her. "What? All the same?" I asked. "All the same," she answered. She was beginning to wax quite tart, as if she didn't want me to have more than my share, as if she thought me greedy, even though the shelves were still groaning with a dazzling array of fertility prognosticators. "Fine, then. I'll just take three," I said, sensing that compromise would have to be brought to bear unless I wanted to do some pretty fancy explaining. I didn't feel like telling her, as probably I ought to have, that when you think you might be on the cusp of parenting the new Messiah you really can't be too careful and seven pregnancy tests is not a superfluity. She slipped my packages of Fact Plus, Answer Now, and Clear Blue Easy into a discreet sack and said, "That comes to $50.79." I paid up and left the store. I couldn't wait to get home and try them out! En route, I paused briefly to buy and swill a litre of mineral water. By the time I got through the door I was fit to bust.

I danced a nervous jig in the kitchen while I opened the boxes. My dog danced along, thinking I might be unwrapping something edible from which she could profit. She jumped up to sniff the thin wand that slid from the Answer Now box, which in its foil wrapping is just the size and shape of an after-dinner mint we both favour. A similar contrivance lived in Clear Blue Easy, while Fact Plus housed no fewer than three tenants: a plastic urine container, an applicator, and a hermetically sealed "test disk."

Each kit came with a long sheet of instructions, and these quickly put the lie to the pharmacist's "all the same" reassurances. While they share a common principle and end (pee, then wait to see if you're knocked up), they are administratively vastly different, one from the other. For instance, only the makers of Answer Now were thoughtful enough to incorporate an "easy grip handle" on their "one step tester." The purveyors of Clear Blue Easy were scrupulous in their own way, providing a cap you can slip onto the "absorbent sampler tip" in order to prevent spotting on the bathroom counter, as well as specific directions that while peeing, one mustn't splash the windows in which the test results are displayed. Although Fact Plus—with its clinical sample cup and its urine dropper and the "test disk" into which the stuff is dripped—is far and away the most cumbersome of the three, it also provides the user with the suitably grave feeling of taking part in a carefully regulated scientific experiment.

I found Answer Now the easiest to use of the three, and its pink answer to my question came up very quickly and distinctly. The robin-egg whispering of Clear Blue Easy took longer to be heard, and was never as clearly articulated. Even though Fact Plus kept me in suspense just a tad too long, and left me with a cup full of cooling pee to deal with, it was the most fun of the three.

My trinity of tests showed a common result. In the fullness of time, all will be revealed. I'm not yet ready to spill the beans. In the interim, if anyone can tell me the name of the English insurance company that will pay 1,500,000 bucks to clients who can prove to have been impregnated by God (cf. Harper's "Index," December 1996), give me a dingle. Late morning is best. Typically, the nausea eases up around 11.

service above and beyond the call

"Number of wooden penises used to demonstrate condoms,
declared surplus by the Saskatchewan department of education
after objections by sex-education teachers: 1000."
—The Globe and Mail's Report on Business magazine

a passel of lads was exceedingly
glad in a bar up in old Saskatoon,
They'd money and time and the jukebox was primed to play
nothing but discothèque tunes.
They were brimming with beans and they sported tight jeans and
their shirts were of various plaids,
They were high, they were spry, they were genial guys, this party
of roustabout lads!

Then out of the dark, which was frigid and stark, and into their
welcoming den,
There stumbled a fellow a long way from mellow, well known to
all of these men.
He was Randy, the flutist. Well—really the truth is that fluting he
worked at by day.
By night he worked hard, a security guard—a dull job, but one
that will pay.

Each evening he toiled, burning bright midnight oil, at a
warehouse a mile down the road,
The place where the school board—those makers of rules—hoard
the stuff that they want to unload:
The old scraps of maps and the inkwells and crap like the busted-
up fragments of chalk,
And the desks and the texts that no longer impress and the
hundreds of used wooden cocks.

It bears out inspection: a thousand erections all lovingly carved
out of oak,

A gross of these sticks made to look just like dicks and whose
    licence they chose to revoke.
It's known through the region a great penile legion now
    languishes under a cloud,
Dreaming of days when they garnered great praise for standing up
    stiff, straight, and proud.

No one can tell how exactly the hell on a day back in August or May,
Some prim, grim trustee or some graver grandee said those
    peckers have now had their day.
For years they were seen in the class called "Hygiene" by
    pubescents who'd gather in throngs,
To giggle and sigh and see condoms applied to a wooden and
    wonderful schlong.

What was the reason they fell out of season? We neither can guess
    nor divine,
Unless they were ruled to be fraudulent tools, declining reclining
    supine.
Their perma-tumescence might teach adolescents that tautness is
    always the norm,
Might mean when they've seen Brother Peter lie lean they'd get all
    depressed and forlorn.

It's sad and it's heinous, that gross of oak penises vanished and
    though we have delved,
We just know the cocks were all stuck in a box and the crate was
    summarily shelved.
But Randy the flutist knows just where the loot is, he watches it
    night after night.
Now far from his post, he was white as a ghost, for he'd just had
    a terrible fright.

"Randy! Come in!" said his buds with a grin, and they poured
    him a tall glass of ale.
"Come on in, have a seat, take some weight off your feet! You're
    looking all pallid and pale."
He slugged back the beer, gave a belch and a leer, and felt the chill
    fear start to thaw.

"Fellas," he said, with a voice full of dread. "Christ! You'll never
believe what I saw!"

"I'll give you my drift. I was working my shift and I needed a lift.
I was blue.
I was feeling depressed when my thoughts coalesced and I
suddenly knew what to do.
I'd reach in and pick out a petrified dick, click my penknife, then
deft and astute,
I'd practise my craft, dig some holes in the shaft, and I'd carve me
a sweet little flute.

"Alone in my palace I hauled out a phallus and gripping it tight in
my hands
I hacked at the pole, gouged the requisite holes, and I hollowed it
up to the glans.
Lord, but how festive it felt to molest it! Suffused with artisanal glow
And eager for succour I tested my pucker. My God, I was itching
to blow!

"I blew and I blew and my confidence grew and the music just
flew round the room:
Waltzes and hornpipes, my all-but-forlorn pipe dispelling all
traces of gloom.
I piped and I played! It was grand! It was gay! Of a moment I
happened to glance
Back at the crate where the dicks lay in state and I saw they were
starting to dance.

"I mean it! I've seen it! A thousand wood penises—really a
thousand less one—
Had jumped from their crate in excitable state and were starting
to join in the fun.
They twisted and turned, they were febrile, they burned. In short,
I would say overall
I've never observed such a fun-loving herd as penises having a ball.

"And then in a flash they all made a great dash for the window
and everyone jumped!

My God! It was stunning! They hit the ground running and off
    down the pavement they humped!
That whole flock of cocks scuttled right down the block, those
    thousand less one six-inch spears,
They capered, cavorted, they scuttled and sported. In seconds,
    they'd plumb disappeared."

Then Randy collapsed, gave his last rasping gasp, he clasped at his
    chest and expired.
His friends shook their heads. They were sad he was dead. In
    delusion he'd plainly been mired.
They pooh-poohed his tale while those snippets of males were
    leaving them all in the dust:
By next morning at eight, when they hopped on a freight, they
    were singing, "To Dildo—or bust!"

see also jane

*News Item: The American Urological Association recently unveiled the
results of a study into penis length conducted by researchers at the
University of California, San Francisco. They examined 60 healthy
males and found that, on average, the penis when erect measured
5.1 inches in length and 4.9 inches in circumference.*

---

*Excerpts from the private journal of Claudia S.,
formerly a researcher at the University of California, San Francisco.*

Dec. 28/94

After months of unemployment,
received phone call from lab at U. Cal, offering job measuring
penises. Was so overjoyed I sang "Pennies from Heaven" to project
supervisor over the phone. Modified the words only slightly in a
way I thought she might find amusing. Cool silence over the line.
Oh, well! Start in New Year. Can't wait!

Jan. 7/95
Training completed. Today, we began measuring Ernest in earnest. Supervisor placed notes in all our mail slots detailing phrases and expressions that are *verboten* in lab. These include "bigger than a breadbox," "give them an inch and they'll take a mile," "home of the whopper," "mightier than the sword," "*oui, oui,*" "the bigger they are, the harder they fall" and "the compass points north." Made the mistake of whistling "He's Got the Whole World in His Hands" in the hallway. Saw supervisor reach for my file. Must be a music hater.

Jan. 25/95
Met with research volunteer Brad W., a healthy male, who had difficulty upholding his end of the experiment. Consulted lab manual for suggestions on how to proceed. "Put subject at ease by chatting informally. Ask him about his work," it said. Couldn't repress urge to point out the irony when Brad reported he was employed by Microsoft. Brad stalked out and blabbed to supervisor. Claimed he felt "deflated." Letter of reprimand added to my file.

Feb. 9/95
Rough day in the lab. Subject Clifford P., impervious to the empirical evidence of impartial numbers, insisted my measurements were at least two inches shy of those he took himself in his basement workshop. Said my tape measure was cold, and that influenced the results. Okay, so maybe I shouldn't have warmed it up in the microwave before repeating the experiment. Salve and bandages deducted from my cheque. Letter of reprimand added to my file.

Feb. 26/95
Reprimanded once again by supervisor, this time for recording information extraneous to experiment. Not scientifically valid to note the names men assign their parts. Made me go through my files with Liquid Paper, excising "Wee Willy Winky," "Curly Joe," "Flopsy," "Mopsy," "Cottontail," and "Peter." Too bad. Feel persuaded this is important data for understanding differences between sexes. After all, I've had my hamster for two years and still just call it "Hamster." Does this mean nothing? Photocopied for my own reference chart of guy who said, "Shake hands with Cedric."

Mar. 8/95
Therapist thinks I might be taking too much of my work home with me. Maybe she has a point. Broke into helpless laughter at a dinner party when someone used phrase "tools of the trade." Guffawed on bus at newspaper story mention of "honourable member." Can hardly speak a sentence that doesn't have a dangling participle. Can't repress giggles when my niece reads from her school primer about Spot, Fluff, Jane, and You-Know-Who. Late to the lab this morning. Supervisor made a note in my file.

Mar. 29/95
Arrested in Safeway this p.m. for arranging bananas and oranges into patterns offensive to produce manager. Allowed one phone call. Dialled supervisor, hoping she'd post bail. Found myself singing "I've got a loverly bunch of coconuts" and laughing hysterically.

Apr. 25/95
Received call from employment office today offering job selling foot-longs at Candlestick Park. Thinking about it. At least a hot dog won't try to convince you it's really 14 inches.

if i were a gal

i was hanging out with a bunch of gal pals the other night, and I was struck once again by just how much I like them. Gals, that is. In fact, "like" is too weak a word. Let's make that "love." I love gals. As a group. Always have. I know I risk being pilloried here for invoking sweeping generalities, and I know that someone will say, "Yeah? What about Mrs. Thatcher?" But I don't care. By and large, gals are great. I love them for their intelligence, their subtlety, their sensitivity to nuance, their social ease. Gals amaze me, the way they pay attention to each other, the way they listen between the lines, the easy way they have with confidences, their ready access to emotion, the way they're disinclined to belittle others by bagging on about their own accomplishments.

Of course, one of the reasons gals come off so well when we talk about them as a group is because, of necessity, we must compare them to guys. And guys are pigs. We'll all be better off if we just acknowledge this as a fact and that the exceptions only serve to prove the rule. Guys are pigs and gals are swell. Period. What's really amazing is that, in spite of the social revolution of the last quarter-century, gals continue to put up with so much from guys. Why should this be? I can only suppose that it's biologically based tolerance. That's great for guys, the group to which I belong. Nevertheless, I sometimes find myself wondering how I'd try to live my life and change the world, if I were a gal.

If I were a gal, I'd stay home from work when I was having my period. I would. Believe me, any guy who woke up one morning and found that he was oozing blood from between his legs would be screaming for the paramedics. If I were a gal, I'd just pick up the phone and say, "Sorry, I can't come in today, I seem to be bleeding. And I won't be back until it stops." Nor would I try to prove a ridiculous point by plugging myself up with something absorbent and putting on a white tennis skirt. No way! I would stay in bed and read novels by gals, or watch Katharine Hepburn videos. And maybe I'd organize a phone tree with the express purpose of having as many gals as possible call in bleeding on the same day. That's what I'd do if I were a gal.

If I were a gal, I'd spearhead something called National Knee-a-Suit-in-the-Balls Day. Why, even speaking as a guy it makes me crazy to see these self-absorbed, self-important business twits swaggering around downtown in their regulation navy ensembles; these three-piece wonders, laughing into their phones and patting their Sassooned hair, the cel and gel set. Yeesh! Look at them! They think they own the world, and you can bet that the sentiment owes its origin in large measure to the fact that they are guys. I sometimes feel like standing on the street corner and passing them leaflets that say, "Has it occurred to you that you've lived over half your life and soon you will be dead?" It would be a kindness to do something to relieve them of their guyish smugness. If I were a gal, I'd capitalize on the fact that they carry their genitalia externally, and it hurts like hell if the equipment gets thwacked, even just a little bit. Ever see a look of pain pass over a guy's face when he crosses his legs too quickly? That's why! It would do these assholes good to get a wee nudge in the groin from a gal, just to remind them of their own vulnerability. That's what I'd do, if I were a gal.

If I were a gal, I'd foment revolution in theatre lobbies. Why should gals have to stand twitching in an intermission line-up that snakes halfway across the lobby, waiting for a chance to pee, while guys can just whistle in and out like nobody's business? Could it be because the facilities were planned by other guys? Maybe! If I were a gal, I don't think I'd be so patient. I think I'd stampede the men's room. And believe me, speaking as a guy, I can say that I'd far rather use a toilet after a gal, since guys as a species think it's beneath them to wipe their own urine off the toilet rim. This is a fact, and no amount of university education can change this or induce more savoury habits.

If I were a gal, I think I'd lobby to have something done about reproduction. Oh, I know, I know, there are some who say that drawing a fully gestated child out of your very own loins is a psychosexual experience and just the greatest thing, but I feel sure that they have merely bought some fringe party line. I have seen a baby being born, and I understand why it's called labour. It's like trying to get a nine-pound turkey out of an eggcup. Let's tell it like it is. Nature is not all it's cracked up to be. Mistakes were made along the way, and the system is well and truly fucked up. There has to be a better way. So, if I were a gal, I'd campaign to see if there wasn't something that could be done with Velcro implants to make the whole exercise a bit more straightforward. Rip, rip, yank out a baby: what could be simpler? On the other hand, I like gals so much that if I were a gal, I'd be a lesbian, and I'd run in the opposite direction whenever someone so much as whispered the word "baster." So for me, it wouldn't really matter.

This is what I'd do, if I were a gal. Which I plan to be in my next incarnation, scheduled for the year 2137. And believe me, if by then things aren't a hell of a lot different for gals on earth, then there's gonna be big, big trouble.

cast of three with noises off

"One night a few of us, shall we say, lesbians, were all in the hot tub watching the guys play basketball in the pool. We were staring at Brad, and we all agreed he could change a woman's mind."

—Singer Melissa Etheridge, discussing hunk-of-burning-love movie star and cover boy Brad Pitt in *Vanity Fair*, February 1995

S O A K I N G: A Play in One Naughty Act

Somewhere in southern California. Melissa, Kathy Dawn, and Lily are in a hot tub, immersed up to their necks. They pass binoculars back and forth, surveying an off-stage swimming pool invisible to the audience. Noises off: boys being buoyant. The time, unfortunately, is now.

Kathy: Wow! Oh, wow! Just take a gander at that! Good golly Miss Molly! Something's shifting in my brain! Until today I'd always thought of a hot tub as a place to relax and hang out with my gal pals. I never really thought of it as the perfect arena from which to watch the fellas shoot a few hoops.
Lily: No kidding! What changed your mind?
Kathy: Not what! Who! It was Brad, of course. Brad Pitt changed my mind. *(shouts)* Sink one for me, Brad! Atta boy!
Melissa: Yup. That's Brad for you. I've always said, he's the kind of guy who can change a woman's mind, and change it in a flash, too. I used to have firm convictions about everything. I mean, I was an intellectual Gibraltar.
Lily: That's right. I remember those days.
Melissa: But since meeting Brad, I've changed my mind about *Roe v. Wade*, iced tea, Al Gore, the Mexican economic crisis, wire-haired dachshunds, and I can't even remember what else. Spend half an hour with Brad and you're pretty much guaranteed a complete ideological make-over.
Lily: That's for sure. I know just what you're talking about. Take today, for instance. Before I settled into this hot tub, I'd always thought of a swimming pool as a place best suited to practising the

Australian crawl and the elementary backstroke. Now I see how narrow I've been. Thanks to Brad, I understand that a swimming pool can be much, much more than a damp forum for aquatic activity.

Melissa: Yeah. But who but Brad would ever have pegged it for a basketball court?

Lily: He's a genius! He sees through the mundane! I'm a different woman because of him. (*shouts*) Hey, Brad! You changed my mind! Thanks for keeping me intellectually lively!

Kathy: I don't think he heard you.

Melissa: Water in the ears. It's a liability.

Lily: Look! Look! Brad's getting out of the pool! What's he doing now?

Kathy: Eating a pizza, I think.

Melissa: Omigod! Now he's diving back in! And I always thought you had to wait at least half an hour after eating before going in the water in order to avoid cramps. (*shouts*) Thanks, Brad! Now I know better!

Lily: My horizons are expanding so fast I think they're going to rip in half! Did I ever tell you about the time Brad completely brought me round to his understanding of Mozart during an intermission of *Così fan tutte*? I mean, girls! We are talking paradigm shift! It still makes my thighs tingle.

Kathy: Oooooh! Don't! How much mind-changing can one woman stand in a single afternoon?

Melissa: I know! I know! I feel like I'm losing touch with gravity. Stop it, Brad! Stop it! Stop messing with my mind!

Lily: Heaven help me! Do I look any different? It's happened to me this very second! Brad has just changed my mind about wearing leopard-skin bikini briefs!

Kathy: Catch up, girl! My mind has been changed in that regard for at least half an hour.

Melissa: Mine too. But I still think it's a pretty weird place to pack an eggplant. I mean, why can't he just use a Safeway bag, like all the rest of us?

Lily: 'Cause he's not like the rest of us, sweetheart.

Kathy: He marches to a different drum!

Lily: He's a dude!

Melissa: He's a mensch!

Melissa, Kathy, and Lily together: He's Brad! And he can make a woman change her mind!

(Sound of a ball dribbling, in more ways than one. Fade to black.)

bigger than a cake box

The next-to-last time someone yelled what might have been an insult at me in the street was about six years ago, in Winnipeg. I was bringing a cake to some celebratory occasion. The cake was in a box, and I was carrying it by the string. I put it to you that no one can look masculine while carrying a cake box by a string. No one.

So, I didn't take it too hard when some bad boys driving by in something rusty rolled down their windows and yelled, "Faggot!" as they thundered past. At least, I think that's what they yelled. Their muffler needed fixing, and it might have been "Bag it!" Or "Drag it!" Or even "Gag on it!" But I think it was "Faggot." It all happened so quickly that I couldn't even tell for sure whether it was unkindly meant. Perhaps they were just so excited to see a living, breathing, and walking faggot in their near vicinity that they couldn't stop themselves from vocalizing. I've noticed how birders do this when they sight an exotic specimen.

"Ruby-throated hummingbird!"

"Pileated woodpecker!"

"Faggot!"

It's not so very different.

I'd forgotten all about this until the other day. The Man and I were walking arm in arm, European-style, down Pendrell Street. It was dusk. We passed by a construction site where, despite the relative lateness of the hour, there were still men at work. I went on the alert, as I always do in such a situation, because I want to have a witty rejoinder at the ready in case someone should whistle at me.

No one whistled. Rather, a worker wearing an unhappy combination of plaids stepped into the street and trilled out, "Cocksuckers!" We didn't respond, so he said it again, "Cocksuckers!"

He had a slight speech impediment that rendered his r's into w's. It was cute, really, a little like being accosted by Elmer Fudd. Even so, I was left with the distinct impression that his intentions weren't benign; also that "cocksuckers" was almost certainly the first poly-syllabic word to have passed his lips in many months.

Luckily for him, I'm not the hand-to-hand combat type. I prefer to stun an opponent with verbiage. But I really couldn't think how to answer him. Oh sure, I could have spun about on my pretty little heel and hissed, "Takes one to know one," or "So's your old man," or "Lick a dog's ass till it bleeds, motherfucker," or some such pleasantry. But what would have been the point in that? There would still be the same number of dickheads on the planet. The world would be no less violent a place. My gastric juices would be needlessly stirred up. And as the Man seemed similarly disinclined to engage him in dialogue, we simply shrugged, pressed on, had a pleasant dinner with some friends, went home, slept, and dreamed untroubled dreams.

Funny, how anger can sneak up on you. The very next day, passing the construction site again, I saw what I recognized as the vile man's plaid jacket hanging on a nail. I stared at it for a full minute, imagining how I might put a match to it, or spit on it, or spirit it away to the nearest dumpster. But it looked so forlorn and worn and slack and out of date—so much like its owner, really—I was moved to sadness, rather than vengeance. I was so pleased at the depth of my own compassion that I skipped straight away to the nearest bakery, bought a big cake, and carried the box home by the string. I considered demonstrating my forgiving nature by passing by the construction site again and offering you-know-who a big slice with a rose on it and everything. Then I heard my mother speak in my ear. "Fuck that noise!" she said, just as she did when I was a child. So I had my cake, and ate most of it, too.

earthquake readiness: 1

it is terribly late or very early, depending on your outlook and habits. I've been wakened from a deep, blank sleep by the tandem twitching of my dog, on my left flank, and my lover, on my right. I lie there, staring through the dark, blank space that separates me from the ceiling, and reflect that while this nocturnal choreography is inconvenient, it is nevertheless miraculous in the mutuality of its execution.

The dog, who is positioned so that her bottom is unsettlingly close to my face, drums on my ribs with her four strong feet and makes small, strained grunting noises. What is she chasing? Rabbits? Squirrels? I turn my attention to the Man, who has been kicking me about the shins. Now, he is not only vibrating. He has started to mutter with a sort of Pentecostal enthusiasm. I listen closely, selfishly hoping he might say something revelatory: something about his past, something about his deeper intentions, something complimentary about *me*, perhaps.

Much to my disappointment, I understand nothing. He seems to be speaking in tongues: clicks and whirrs, and random glottal expostulations. Is it a secret lingo of his own devising? The language of lost Atlantis? In the midst of this confusing syllabic hash, a familiar cluster of morphemes insinuate themselves. I hear clearly the word "earthquake." He says it again and again, with mounting panic.

The Man, who is relatively new to these hereabouts, is from a part of the country where the ground is reliable, and disinclined to rupture. I can only suppose his subconscious has chosen this night to process the information that he has come to a more capricious piece of the earth; that at any moment, the tectonic plates might butt heads and wreak havoc everywhere.

My every protective instinct has been aroused. I want to wrap my arms around him, hold him close, and fill his uneasy brain with ludicrous reassurances. I want to say: Rest easy, my love. With me you have nothing to fear. I have learned all there is to learn from the many pamphlets that have been written about this very subject by experts in civil defence.

Routes of egress from blighted urban areas are etched in my brain. There is bottled water in the kitchen, as well as a great many tins of foodstuff, including condensed milk. I have a flashlight, and a battery-operated radio. I will guide you away from fallen high-tension wires. I will lie with you under the table, or hug you close to me in the sheltering arch of a sturdy door frame, and prevent you from giving in to the sensible impulse to rush out of doors as soon as the first trembling has stopped. We will huddle together, for days if necessary, enjoying the aftershocks while waiting for rescue to come. I have the finest insurance policy money can buy. Let me be your shield, your armour, your cushion against grief.

These are all the things I want to murmur, into his ear, into his troubled head. Before I have a chance, the dog's dreams take a startling turn, and she yelps, sharply. The Man opens his eyes with a start. He half sits, grunts, looks around with something like recognition, and then collapses into sleep once more. Both he and the dog seem to have found peace. Their six legs are still.

I lie there, still caught up in my little romance of invented catastrophe. Listening to my two companions' regular breathing, I give way to quieter, if no less self-aggrandizing, imaginings. Now I cast myself as the strong but silent guardian of their peace: a minor god or lesser angel charged with their safekeeping. I start to feel dozy and smug: a good combination.

Outside, autumn deepens. A drunk passes beneath the window. He says, to no one in particular, "Fuckin' fags, fuckin' homos, I hate these fuckin' fags." The foghorns start in with their familiar, seasonal bleating: *For-lorn. For-lorn.*

My mother always told me not to drift off while keeping company with nasty thoughts. But one last scrap of intelligence grabs hold as sleep takes me hostage: that the sun will shortly rise on a world of distant and present dangers, and there's not a goddamn thing I can do about any of them.

where to find it

a few blocks from the house where I grew up, a short bicycle hop away, lived a guy called Frank. Frank was usual in every way. Middle-aged. Middle class. Altogether average. He kept his house neat, and he kept his lawn trim, and you would never have pegged him as the type to murder his wife and bury her body in the back garden.

Weeks went by. The neighbours asked after her whereabouts. They were neither discomfited nor suspicious when he told them she'd been summoned back to Germany on family business. A few of them felt sorry for this unassuming man who was having to "bach it." They invited him for dinner. They brought him casseroles. Had it not been for the dog next door exhibiting a new enthusiasm for digging in Frank's garden, his crime might never have been discovered.

The police swarmed in and out of the place for a couple of days; then it sat empty. For weeks afterward, whenever we rode our bicycles down Frank's street—and somehow, we always managed to chart a route that would take us in that direction—there would always be gawkers on the sidewalk, staring at that stucco bungalow. It was as unremarkable as its owner, but it had taken on a kind of totemistic poetry. People came from all over the city to contemplate it, as though it were a weeping Virgin or a speaking oracle. They watched it for hours on end. You might have thought they expected it to lift off, or self-immolate, or suddenly change colour.

Frank was tried and found guilty. Before he'd served one year of his sentence, he hanged himself in his cell. Time passed. Someone bought the house. The dog who made the discovery died. The casserole dishes Frank had warmed in his oven and dutifully returned were broken, or sold at yard sales. Frank slipped from our minds. But in recent days, he has insinuated his way into the folds of my brain. I can't imagine why, except it seems to have been a week diminished by more than a usual number of instances of Hannah Arendt's "banality of evil."

In our myths and nightmares, evil is easy to portray and to know. It comes with all kinds of markers: horns, warts, stinking breath, black Stetsons, fiery eyes. But Frank was just a shuffling guy who'd help you jump-start your car and who kept the sidewalk clear of snow. He wouldn't stand out in a crowd any more than Susan Smith, whose picture has been in the papers every day this week. We see her, peering back at us from behind her round glasses. If we didn't know her circumstances, didn't know her to be the convicted murderer of her two sons, she might just as easily be a distracted woman on a packed bus, casting about hopefully for a seat. And here are Lorelei and Steven Turner, coming down the steps of the courthouse in Miramichi, N.B., assailed by jeering spectators appalled that the couple allowed their three-year-old son to starve, but who in the photographs look for all the world as if they're wondering whether or not they remembered to turn off the oven before going to the grocery store. And in St. Catharines, the Cape Cod house that was once the home of Paul Bernardo attracts a steady stream of tourists. It is ordinary in its every outward aspect and has nothing to reveal about the awful whys of the murders alleged to have happened within.

A house gets sprayed with graffiti: "You'll pay Paul." Fists are shaken outside a courthouse. A mob clamours for a young woman's death. The victims, we say, must be avenged and we vent our anger, ostensibly on behalf of the dead and the maimed. But I wonder how much of our outrage is rooted in the fear we bring to the violation of ordinariness; in the evidence that evil is not extraordinary and removed but quotidian and, yes, even banal; that it chooses people who look just like us as its cuckoo nest.

"He seemed so normal," Frank's neighbours told the reporters. Nothing would ever be the same.

fairytale

Two sad stories made headlines at roughly the same time. In Saskatchewan, Robert Latimer rigged a hose to the exhaust pipe to end the life of his severely disabled daughter, Tracy, while she sat in the cab of his truck. In South Carolina, Susan Smith sent her car rolling into a lake and drowned her sons, who were trapped inside. This piece was suggested by the coincidence of these two tragedies, and by the evident differences between them.

These things happened.

A woman strapped her two pretty babies in her car, and sent it rolling into the lake. They drowned.

In another country, a sad man shut his suffering daughter in the cab of his truck and piped it full of exhaust. She died.

These things happened, and I think of them.

I think of them and I write them down.

I write:

One car.

One truck.

Two countries.

Two parents with their several reasons.

Three children.

Three deaths.

These things happened and I write them down like an equation. As if they could be stretched on the rack of a formula, and made to make sense. As if they could be balanced. As if there's a point of intersection where there will be clarity. But it doesn't matter how I turn or twist or measure them. I can't make them fit. Sense cannot be wrung from them; only the certainty that these things happened.

These things happened, and when we hear of them we recoil. We recoil to think of the children. The innocent boys, the pain-wracked girl, the end of their breathing. We recoil when we think "flesh of their flesh." And we recoil because stories like these make us inhabit the mind of the murderer, which turns out to be our own mind. We learn this when we fill in the blanks, which we can't help but do. We can't help but wonder what they thought and felt. That man. That woman. How did it feel to lay the plans, to tell the lie, to assemble the hardware, to pull the brake, to connect the tubes, to see the car roll off with its awful freight, to turn the truck into a gas chamber?

And of course, we know. We know exactly how that feels. We can imagine so easily the fear, the confusion, the shaky resolve, the terrible knowing that soon it will be too late, the moment when there is no chance of reprieve, the sickening knowledge that it's done, the silence that ought to go on forever. Maybe there's a feeling of accomplishment. Maybe there's a second of exultation.

Is it so hard to imagine these things? No. These things live in all of us. So does the possibility that that man's and that woman's strength, or nerve, or desperation, or madness, might usurp the throne of our reason. We know what they felt, and any one of us might easily do what they did. This is a risk of being human. We are flesh of their flesh. And these things happen.

This happened, too, once upon a time.

Once upon a time, a brother and a sister lived with their mother and father on the edge of the forest. As there was a famine in the land and the family had no food to eat, the parents conspired to lead the children into the woods and leave them there. The children overheard their parents plotting. The next day, when they went into the forest, they made sure to toss pebbles behind them, in order to mark their path. Their parents lit a fire for them, and said they were going off to gather a few berries. They'd soon return, they promised. Then, they deserted them. And they thought they had seen the last of their children. But that night, when the moon rose, the scattered pebbles shone, and the children found their way home again. The very next day, their parents once again marched them into the woods. This time, they scattered bread crumbs. Night came. The moon rose. But there was no trail. The birds had eaten the crumbs. The children wandered deeper and deeper into the forest. And they were never seen again. Witches, lions, avalanche. Who can say? They were never seen again.

How could such a thing happen? Some say it was because the father couldn't abide watching his little ones, the flesh of his flesh, die a lingering, hungry death. Better to dispatch them to the mercies of the animals of the forest. Some said, no. It was because the mother had gone mad herself with hunger of one kind or another, and couldn't stand to have the morsel of life that was left to her devoured by these two needy, clinging babies. Once she'd made up her mind, it was a cinch. The forest was so close. It was a dark and terrible place. It was exactly the sort of place where these things happened. And in the end, that was all anyone could find to say. Once, they said, there were these children. Then, there were none. It was tragic. It was heartbreaking. It was incomprehensible. It was all these things. Nothing could make it better. There was nothing more to say. These things happened.

what someone should have said

There is this woman. She is in the Safeway parking lot. She is young, maybe 25. She is big, both tall and fat. She looks strong. She is native. She is this big, strong native woman and she does three things at once while people watch, there in the Safeway parking lot. With sharp, hard jerks she smashes the passenger door of her serviceable mid-size car against the driver's side of the sporty little convertible angled next to hers. At the same time, she drags her child out and onto the pavement, hauling him by his hair. And she hollers, loud.

Fuck get the fuck out of the car get the fuck out fuck get the fuck out and get the fuck over there look at the fuckin' mess you've made get the fuck away from me I don't fuckin' want you near me.

She shoves him backwards. He bawls and staggers into the middle of the lot where he continues the vomiting he began in the car. He is awash with tears, and covered with his own orange puke, wasted junk food. He is five. Maybe six. The woman redirects her rage at another child—his sibling?—who is just visible in the back seat.

Don't just fuckin' sit there clean up that fuckin' mess go on you fuckin' start cleaning it up.

By now there are more onlookers, a small cluster. Everyone gapes. A man steps forward. He is half her size. She towers over him, diminishes him with her bulk and her rage. He is a slight Asian man. He gestures helplessly at the sports car, the one she has been smashing. His car. He cannot believe what he is seeing. No one can. She looks down at the chipped paint, the dents. She asks, how much do you want? She folds her mighty arms across her chest and talks in three directions at once, venting her wrath in an omnidirectional spray.

So how much do you want to fix it tell me how much you shut up and stay over there you just fuckin' keep away from me you clean that up why should you see my licence just tell me how much.

She is nervous now. Everyone can see that, which makes her want to hide it the more. She gets louder.

Well how should I know how much why don't you ask someone?

This all happens in the space of a couple of minutes, although those minutes are so elastic they mimic hours. More than a dozen people are gathered watching now, maybe twice that many peer from the windows of the supermarket, peer from behind the signs advertising the price of asparagus. Everyone waits for someone to do something. No one moves. Everyone is estranged from action, caught in a web of embarrassments and imaginings. Embarrassed somehow that it's a native mother carrying on like this, and not a well-heeled white woman. Imagining how she would behave without the softening influence of an audience. Embarrassed by her anger. Imagining the home life of the children. Embarrassed that the car is being fussed over, the children ignored. Imagining the fates that will befall these kids ten years hence. Embarrassed by this show of collective ineptitude, embarrassed by this stupid paralysis, this reeling backward in the face of the woman's fury. Imagining the consequences of calling social services, imagining the consequences of not calling. No one knows the right thing to do. No one is competent here. And isn't this just the way it always is when there are innocent, injured creatures who require tending?

Later that night, when they are at home, when they are lying in bed, all these people will remember what happened, will think on it, will turn it over and over it in their heads. All over the neighbourhood, people will be waiting for sleep and thinking, "I should have. . ."

"I should have walked right up to her and said, now listen here, lady, you can't treat your children like that! Lay off! That's what I should have said!"

"I should have said to her, you must have been having a really bad day. Why don't you take a few deep breaths and cool down for a few minutes? I'll look after the kids."

"I should have called the cops. Those kids need to be apprehended."

"I should have said, I'll clean the car, you clean up your son."

"I should have gone to that little boy . . ."

". . . should have held him . . ."

". . . should have wiped him off . . ."

". . . shouldn't have worried about getting puke on my suit."

"I should have just—just—well—I shouldn't have stood there."

"I should have known what to do."

The native woman and the Asian man somehow settle their business. She grabs the crying child by the hand and hustles him into the fetid car. She guns the engine and wheels it out of the lot and turns east onto Broadway. Someone picks up the pay phone and dials 911 and tells whoever answers something of what has happened, reports that the licence number is AJS—, receives some kind of reassurance, hangs up, sticks her finger in the coin return slot, finds a quarter, pulls it out. What a world. Always, there's someone who wins.

everything it carries away

a few weeks ago, I flew from the West Coast to the prairies, and when I was nearly home, I looked down on the floods. Unaccustomed as I am to interpreting the mind of a river from 35,000 feet, I'm not sure I would have recognized the field-wrecking insurrection for what it was, were it not for prior knowledge acquired through news reports. From my lofty vantage point, it looked to me as though the normally placid Assiniboine was content to divide its liquid assets between two safe banks and keep its counsel.

My father picked me up at the airport. We are a little tentative with each other when we meet after a time apart. That's our way. By the time we'd reached the car (which, for some reason, he has started calling "the Vehicle"), we'd exhausted all our conversational set pieces. Luckily, there was the river to fall back on. True, it has heaped the bulk of its indignities on rural Manitoba and Saskatchewan. Nevertheless, it is this self-same river that runs right through the middle of Winnipeg, only a few blocks from the house where I grew up and where my parents still live. I felt sure there must be tales to tell of near misses, of washed-out sidewalks, and of knee-deep basements.

Flood stories were among the narrative staples of my childhood. In fact, my brothers and I learned from an early age about the close link between diluvian drama and the mythology of our own beginnings. How our parents were married in the midst of the great Winnipeg flood of May 1950, when the combined anger of the Red and the Assiniboine threatened to wash the whole city away, was an oft-told tale.

Even now, when I look at the pictures of that big day, I think of all the stories: of how my grandparents were late because they had to drive 20 miles out of the city to find a place to cross the river; of the last-minute change of venue because the church was submerged; of how my father was heaving sandbags against the advancing water only an hour or two before his own wedding. I look at the photo of them getting into the decorated car after the service, my mother in her fairytale dress, my father in his new suit, and think of them hurrying to board their plane for Minneapolis. The river is only hours away from cresting, but they, like all newly-weds, simply had to trust that everything would work out for the best. I think of them looking down from those unfamiliar heights on what they knew to be the flood, but seeing just the slow amble of the green-grey river following its own path south.

By the time they returned, the crisis was over. They bought a house for about the same price they paid for the Vehicle they now drive. My father hammered a nail into one of the beams in the basement and hung up his sandbagging hip-waders. They were still there, the last time I thought to check.

"Been down to look at the river?" I asked brightly, as the ignition turned over.

"River?" he asked, seemingly surprised that I would pull such a question randomly from out of the air. "No. Not recently."

"I just thought that with the flood and all . . ."

"Oh! The river," he said, as though he had suddenly remembered this as something we once shared. "The flood. No."

We settled into a silence that shifted, as it always does, from awkward to companionable. At home, he parked the Vehicle and carted one of my bags into the house, not even looking to the south where the dangerous river rolled and rumbled, challenging its margins. It made me sad to see how he turned his back on the flood; sadder still to see in his forsaking the foreshadowing of how I will one day do the same. Not now, though. For now, and for as long as I'm able and as long as I care, I will be the guardian of that boisterous roiling, and the keeper of what it means and meant. All that night, I lay in bed and imagined it. I could scarcely sleep for thinking of everything it was carrying away.

"do not leave child unattended"

as a very young child, I was riddled with all the usual abandonment anxieties. I fretted that I would wake in the morning to find my mother and father gone;

that they would fly away under cover of dark, or fail to return from a party and leave me in the clutches of Helen, the chain-smoking baby-sitter who was evil incarnate. I worried that on a family outing to the near-by park—where it was part of our routine for my father to hoist me onto the thick, concrete railing of the bridge so I might watch the rolling of the river underneath—that I would be allowed to fall and would be carried away on the current, junior jetsam, like Moses consigned to the rushes, only not so dry, and probably not so lucky, come the end of the day. But nowhere did these fears of desertion or betrayal find so sharp a focus as in the supermarket shopping cart.

I should say that both my parents were paragons of responsibility. They took their obligations seriously. They held us in high regard, in the truest sense of the word. They kept a close eye on us. They were vigilant for anything that looked like a sign of miscreant behaviour. Neither my mother nor my father could abide children careening out of control, tearing along the aisles of the Serv Well Supermarket, which was where they shopped. They kept us smartly in line through such expedient means of confinement as the fold-down kiddy seat that is part of the familiar equipment of any shopping cart. I can see myself now, a fledgling in that shallow metal nest, my tubby legs extended through its apertures, nursing the worry that this would be the day my mother would look at her grocery list, make a pretence of having forgotten some sales item one aisle over, excuse herself for 20 seconds while she went to retrieve it, and then disappear, just walk out the door and down the street, walk into the sunset, leaving me with no dowry other than some thawing pork chops and a box of Shreddies.

Honestly! When I look back on the tremulous mess I was as a child, I'll never understand how I achieved the firm and self-actualized foundation to which I can now lay claim. I will say, however, that I've latterly had a demonstration of the way the roots of neuroticism can push their shoots up through the most marmoreal resolve, in that once again the abstract prospect of abandonment and the tangible presence of shopping carts have united to cast a shadow over my days. For reasons that may have to do with malice aforethought, or may be nothing more than dumb coincidence, the sidewalks and laneways in my neighbourhood have latterly been strewn with more than the usual number of these helpful conveyances. The other day, I counted seven on my way to the Sky-Train station. Seven, for heaven's sake, and in just a three-block span! Of course, I considered the possibility that it might be a performance piece, a public installation sanctioned by the city and sustained by a grant-giving agency. I hoped, briefly, that they had once contained the possessions of a squad of street people who had managed to find safe and affordable housing and therefore no longer required these portable lockers. But I think it more likely that the carts were the cast-offs of care-for-nothing fuckers who used them to wheel their purchases home from the nearby Safeway, and then left them to clutter the public thoroughfares.

Seven shopping carts! Abandoned! It made me furious to see them. Irrationally furious! What's more, they put me on the express lane to regression. All the bogeys of childhood came out of the shadows and danced around, hooting and jibing and rattling their chains. By the time I got to the station, I was a thumb-sucking wreck. So much that was grievous, so much that was emblematic of everything that is rotten about the human condition was embodied in those porous, vacant carts. The absolution of responsibility. The failed promise of abundance. The shrugging ease with which we turn our backs. Our willful blindness. Our dangerous rationalizations. Our pouting reluctance to deal with someone else's carelessness—for would it not have been simple enough for me to have pushed a cart or two back to the Safeway rather than to leave them there, with the empty wind whistling through the metal grille of their skeletons? "Accccchhhh," I said, out loud, as the train pulled away, and the crowd of commuters stepped back, as if to give me air.

It was a relief when I returned home, quite late that evening, to find that the carts were gone, repatriated I imagine. The prodigals had returned home, eager to receive the fatted calf, the tin of salmon, the box of pasta, whatever. They were all gone save one. It was under the elevated track, nestled against a far trestle, half-obscured from view. A single crow gripped the push bar. You didn't have to be an ornithologist to see that this was not a well bird. Its hold was tenuous at best. It rocked back and forth like a yeshiva boy over his studies. Its eyes were glazed. It was past caring about shiny things. Clearly, it had cawed its last. It was preparing to croak. What better place to prepare itself for abandonment? Crows are social. To see just one portends sorrow. That's what an old superstition tells us, and this sad sight bore out the truth of it, this tattered old thing on a half-rusted buggy, consigned to a far corner, articulating the dusk. I woke up in the middle of the night and wondered if it was over. In the morning, there was not a sign of crow or of cart. That was the kind of morning it was. Nowhere, no matter where you looked, was there evidence of anything like abandonment.

sunday afternoon optimism

The doorbell rang. It was Sunday afternoon. I was just home. I had been out marketing. I was putting away the groceries. Dry goods in the cupboards. Veggies in the fridge. For generations, my family has handled groceries in this arcane way. Don't ask me why. It's just the way we've always done it. The doorbell rang as I was holding a chilled plastic bag at arm's length. I had taken it from the fridge. I was squinting at its contents, a viscous, greenish goop. It had been in the fridge a long time. It had been there since the last time I went marketing, which was some weeks back. I can only market on days when my reservoir of good cheer is full to brimming. Otherwise, I am paralysed by a combination of too many choices and terrible lighting.

That morning—it was a Sunday, as I think I've mentioned—I'd woken up full of optimism. The sun shone. My breath was minty. The birds sang. If you were expecting a diagnosis, you'd want to hear from your doctor on just such a day. Nothing could go wrong. All the indicators suggested that not even a trip to Safeway would go amiss. And it was so. Everything went tickety-boo. I got home safe and sound. I opened the cupboards. I opened the fridge. The slime in the bag—I think it was once a lettuce—was the one worm in an otherwise fragrant bud. Nasty slime!

The doorbell rang. I was glad to hear it. It provided a distraction. I have spent far too many hours of my one-and-only life trying to work out just exactly why the hell the thing is called a crisper when "oozer" would be so much more apt. Ding-dong went the bell. I opened the door, just wide enough to stick my head out. You can never be too cautious. You can never tell when it might be a gang, intent on stealing your jewels. Such things happen, even in quiet neighbourhoods such as mine. Even on Sunday afternoons such as this.

A man and a woman were on the stoop. They were older, and nicely dressed. He was tall. She was not. They seemed very respectable. I sensed that from them I had nothing to fear. For one thing, they had quite nice jewelry already, as nice as anything they'd find at my house. And they carried clipboards. I always find a clipboard reassuring, particularly if it's accessorized with a lab coat. My visitors weren't wearing lab coats, but I was still able to find it in my heart to trust them. They said they were doing a survey of Catholics in the parish. "Parish" is a word I find unsettling, if only for homophonic associations. I didn't tell them this, for which I'm now sorry. It might have led to quite an interesting discussion, possibly about life after death, a concept which terrifies me. What's the point of death if it only leads to more life? If only I'd thought to ask, they might have cleared a few things up for me. They told me they were doing a survey and they looked at me, meaningfully, and with an air of expectation.

"Not Catholic," I said. I was quite tightlipped. I'd been eating some of the celery I'd purchased while marketing. I feared there might be a strand stuck between my teeth. This is the risk of celery, which is unfortunate, since it is an excellent source of roughage. I believe it also contains a certain amount of natural arsenic, though not enough to harm anyone who eats it in moderation. Which I do. Anyway, with Albania in turmoil and Clifford Olson asking for parole there is more to worry about than the possibility of celery poisoning, n'est-ce pas? Where was I? Oh, yes. I kept tightlipped because of the strand possibility and because I could tell they were nice people. They were Catholics, with modest but attractive jewels, clipboards, and no lab coats, but with the best of intentions. I didn't want to embarrass them or put them in the position of having to decide whether or not they should point out my vege-dental gaffe. Even good friends hesitate to break such ugly news. I recently spent an entire afternoon with a morsel of pizza sausage congealing on my cheek. Everyone around me was too delicate to point it out, even though I would have been glad to know and wouldn't have been angry in the slightest way. It was worse for them than it was for me. That nubbin of stray sausage must have caused them great distress. I felt badly to have been the source of their angst. I would have been mortified to put my unbidden visitors, strangers to me, through that same fretful soul-searching, especially on a Sunday afternoon when they'd just been to Mass, and they were out doing good work, and surely felt at peace with the world.

"Not Catholic," I said. "Oh," was their only answer. I thought they looked disappointed. Perplexed. Taken aback, even. They went away. I closed the door. I stepped back inside. I passed the hallway mirror. I opened my mouth to locate the offending fibre. I noted I was sporting my new baseball cap, which I'd completely forgotten. I don't usually wear one in the house. It was a bad-hair-day vanity. The cap—it's green—is emblazoned with the name of Richard Branson's company. "Virgin," it says. Well! No wonder my parish visitors were confused! This explained the weight of their considerate regard. Virgin! Of course! They mistook me for a player! Oh, dear! Well, the joke was on them, even though there are times I think I'd like to be a Catholic, which I might have told them under different circumstances. I look on that Holy Ghost stuff with a certain scepticism, but I do feel I'm missing out on something at Eastertime. Palm Sunday, Maundy Thursday, Good Friday: I'd like it if these days came along and I felt a frisson shinny up my spine, as must my would-be surveyors. It was too late to ask them. They were gone.

All the while, I'd been holding the bag of green slime in my left hand. I looked at it anew and saw in the nick of time that slime is an anagram not just for miles and limes but for smile. Smile! Of course! And to think I was about to get rid of so worthwhile a reminder that nothing is as bad as it seems. So, I put that bag right back in the crisper where I'd found it. That was Sunday afternoon. I have thought of it often between then and now. And I have cracked a big dumbass grin, every single time.

a postal box named desire

Saw you in the Davie Street Safeway, Wednesday, June 22, 5:37 p.m. We were both at the cherry bin, your blond hair swept back in a bad boy pompadour, icy blue eyes, two rings in your right ear, a diamond stud in your left, and a small mole on your chin. You look like River Phoenix. Only healthier. If you know what I mean. You were wearing a tank top and black cycling shorts, and you have a Celtic knot tattooed around your right ankle. Me: brown hair, light stubble on face, wearing jeans (ripped at the knees) and a faded purple Gap T-shirt. I was humming "The Atchison, Topeka and the Santa Fe," since it was the 25th anniversary of the death of Judy Garland, and I never really liked "Over the Rainbow" all that much. In your Breezway basket were three tomatoes, a pork chop, a container of Dutch cleanser, some Freeman skin care products (the apricot and sea kelp scrub, I think), and six tins of Miss Mew tuna and egg cat food. I had half a dozen tins of the same cat food in my basket. It's the only kind my puss will eat. I thought about drawing attention to this coincidence, but didn't. Our fingers brushed as we were picking through the cherries and I almost had to call for oxygen. Wish I'd asked your name. Contact me at 7980.

Dear Box 7980:

I wasn't in the Safeway that day, and I never buy pork chops, and cherries give me the runs, so I guess I'm not the guy you mean. But maybe you can help me out. Did Judy Garland sing "The Atchison, Topeka and the Santa Fe" in *Meet Me in St. Louis* or in *The Harvey Girls*? I'd really like to know, since I've got a bet riding on it. Thanks!

Dear Box 7980:

Did you happen to notice if he had a little gap between his front teeth? Do his eyebrows connect above his nose? I think I used to date that guy, and he's an asshole. He never turns up when he says he's going to, his goddamn cat sheds all over everything, and what's more, he's a lousy lay. He owes me 30 bucks and he still has my copy of Madonna's *Immaculate Collection*, so if you see him again, give him a swift kick in the pills and tell him it's from Darren. By the way, he hates Judy Garland.

Dear Box 7980:

I hope you wash your cherries before you eat them. I know how tempting it can be to snack on a few on the way home from the store. But remember! They've probably been sprayed with horrible chemical agents. Keep safe!

Dear Box 7980:

I once had a cat that only ate chicken livers sautéed in butter and plenty of garlic. Ain't it an amazing world? Call if you like, I'm home most nights!

Dear Box 7980:

Did you notice there was a full moon on June 22? I watched it with my Wicca circle, and we all saw the face of Judy Garland staring out from the Sea of Tranquility. Is it a coincidence that it was 25 years ago this summer, just a month after she died, that man first walked on the moon? I think not! If you're ever out around Commercial Drive and feel like taking one small step, call me!

Dear Box 7980:

Hey Frank! Is this you? It sure sounds like you! You old rascal!

Dear Box 7980:

Congratulations on your search for a meaningful relationship. If you and your intended are ever in need of a good realtor with a solid understanding of the West End market, give me a call! My office will page me, 24 hours a day. Card enclosed.

Dear Box 7980:

Actually, I would have been interested. But just five minutes later, over the eggplants, I met the love of my life. We're moving tomorrow to Calgary, where he has a successful orthodontics practice. At last, I can get my gap narrowed. Sorry, I guess that's life. Best of luck, "River."

five-finger exercise

"Clustering is a nonlinear brainstorming process akin to free association . . . A nucleus word tends to evoke clusters of association."
—Gabriele Lusser Rico, *Writing the Natural Way*

"Complaint." The best thing to be said about "complaint" is that it's orthographically akin to "compliant," but travels in a completely different lane on the highway of meaning. It shares this quality with "united" and "untied," "inner calm" and "intercom," "enrichment" and "in Richmond," "sacred" and "Socred," "*Angles*" and "angels." There are lots of these homonymic antonyms, but why waste a good cluster spelling them all out? Get on with the exercise.

"Summer complaint" was my mother's euphemism for those gutsy surges that overtake us when we succumb to the juicy temptations of too much fresh fruit. Of course, summer complaint was only a possibility when summer was compliant, and the industrious sun had tickled the orchards and gardens into submission, and coaxed them to surrender their treasures: cherries, plums, apricots, nectarines, pears, peaches.

I grew up on the bald prairie and loved all these things: loved them for themselves, and for the boxes in which they travelled, boxes that bore the labels of their distant and exotic points of origin. California. Florida. B.C. Places where the climate was hospitable enough to accommodate their needs and requirements; needs and requirements that were not so very different from my own.

I loved all the fruits of summer, but did not love them equally well. Peaches were my favourite. Peaches were my downfall. Peaches were the apple of my private Eden. I adored them for their Botticelli colour, their sculpted roundness (that seam that made them look like rosy buttocks), their sticky sweetness, their willingness to ooze; adored them even for the hard stone that passed as a heart. I see now that peaches were more than merely a fruit. They were a prophecy of boyfriends to come.

Which brings us to the present day. The Man (whose heart is actually quite mushy, I'm glad to say) and I came back from the market last weekend with three huge California peaches and three avocados. They were not yet ready for devouring, but I had no complaints about the fact that they weren't compliant. They had promising prospects. The afternoon was hot, and in order to hasten their ripening, I placed them on the balcony railing, in the full glare of the July sun.

I sat back and studied them: three avocados, three peaches, each of them slowly softening around the pits that are their sad excuse for a skeleton. They set me to thinking about language. For one thing, they reminded me of punctuation: the peaches like periods, the avocados like apostrophes, ready and waiting in some eccentric printer's tray.

My thoughts drifted to a consideration of how they were resting on a wall: *le mur* in French; and about the odd coincidence that the French for "ripe" is *mûr*. Then I thought about how strange it was that the French have the same word for avocado (*avocat*) as for lawyer; and how peculiar it is that the word for peach (*la pêche*) is remarkably close to the word for sin (*le péché*).

Here were avocados and peaches cheek by jowl, and by simple dint of translation and a bit of stretching they could be transformed to lawyers having a close association with sin! My God! In the heat of the afternoon, it really seemed as if I had stumbled on something, some dark linguistic whisper of the unity that underlies all things. Peaches, avocados, sin, lawyers, ripe, wall: there was something there, something crying out to be grasped and held and understood! I was close! I was oh so very close to being onto something really, really big! Something earth-shaking!

If only I'd been wearing a hat and adequate sunscreen, I would probably have hit the old satori bullseye. Alas, I didn't have the wherewithal, in that heated moment, to really make a grab for it. It slipped between my fingers, like a big and wily fish. My last glimmer of inspiration, in fact, was that "*la pêche*" is also French for "fishing."

There was no point in making any complaint. Within 24 hours, the fruit had grown compliant. I broke the six-part cluster, ate all three peaches in swift succession, and regretted it before the day was out. I looked for consolation in gin. That night, walking the dog past a dry cleaner, I read the word "martinizing" as "Martini Zing!" and sensed once again that I was back on track of putting my ear to the warm and ticking heart of the universe.

the solstice: five postcards

1. These are the days, the very long days, the long very long and lengthening days, the one-turns-into-another days, the proof of the world's revolving days, the soft and warm and evolving days, that soon dissolve in the longest day, the zenith day, the apogee. We dumbly pray the light might stay, but no, oh no, the eager grey that whips the dark is flexed to flay, which makes me say my bets are laid, and it's all downhill from here, my friends, yes it's all downhill from here.

2. Somebody gave us the gift of a nice daisy. You can never really appreciate how nice a gift a daisy makes until you receive one. It came with a name tag. "Osteospermum 'Buttermilk.' African Daisy. Pale yellow to cream on the inside, chocolate cone and striping on the backside of the petals. Best in full sun in a poor but well-drained soil. Ht. 2.' " Others might have been offended at this, but I was not. Not for a second did I imagine our friends wringing their hands in the nice daisy store, all the while saying, "Whatever can we find to take them that will be nice and will thrive in their soil, which is poor but well drained." No, no, no. That was not it at all. I know that they just looked around for something chocolate and something creamy, something with a name that suggests a disease as much as a daisy. "What? Suffering from Osteospermum? A little Buttermilk will fix you up, and all you have to do is swallow." So they bought it and they brought it and we took it from its pot and we put it in the plot where it's pleased with what it's got and its life is far from fraught and it's doing very well, thank you very much for asking, next to the poppies and the snapdragons.

Someday, I'd like to ask the botanist who wrote up the name tag why he or she chose not to reveal the most important of the daisy's qualities, which is that it gets all shy at night. Once the sun goes down, it curls in on itself, draws its pale yellow petals up over its chocolate cone and hides away. Bashful heliotrope! What is it afraid of? The stars? The moon? Is it afraid children will come in the dark and pick it, will run away and dismember it, all in the name of finding out where someone's affections lie? He loves me.

He loves me not. He loves me. He loves me not. Don't be a fool, kid. Everything will change before the summer is over. And anyway, what does a daisy know? What does it know about love? Ask it about being nice. Ask it about being shy. On being nice and on being shy, it is an expert. The world could do with more nice and shy, if you ask me. But like the daisy, I'm old-fashioned. A stick in the mud.

3. In summer, more than in winter, we roamed in packs. Our days were measured by shifting games. They grew one out of the other, with no formal break or line of demarcation. The games changed as the light changed. Tag became Red Rover became Statue became Hide and Seek became Kick the Can became Garden Raid. What did they have in common? They were all about the thrill of capture. The object was to stay free, but the real excitement came when you got caught. To be touched, to be grabbed, to know you were done for, to know there was no escape. This is what you came for, the electric surge, the lurching heart. For what is this a metaphor? Beats me. You figure it out.

4. Where I live, I see mostly the evidence of summertime games rather than the games themselves. Someone, a child, has marked the sidewalk with coloured chalk, has drawn the old pattern of magic squares in their requisite ranks and rows. When first I see that grid, I think that I might dance along it in the old prescribed way. I don't because I half-remember there was a charm you were to say before using someone else's hopscotch, and I have no interest in courting the bad luck that could come my way from that kind of gaffe. And besides, I have shin splints.

I keep a casual eye on the squares for a couple of days, but never see anyone go near them, never see them put to their intended use. Oh, people walk over them, some walk around, but no one ever jumps from one end to another. Then the inevitable rain comes along and writes a hackneyed line at the end of the poem. No one seems to care that the squares are gone. No one ever replaces them.

For an hour or two I agonize over their mythopoeic significance. Then I decide that sometimes a game of hopscotch is just a game of hopscotch.

5. I remember how shocked I was when I had lunch with two women, one from Toronto, one from Vancouver, and learned that neither of them allowed her children to play in the front yard. Too dangerous, they said. You could just never tell who might come along. I asked around and found that this was the norm. That was two years ago, and now I'm so habituated to the idea of danger that I'm shocked when I do see children playing in front of their houses. Like the other night. It was after ten, and the sky was passing from amber to charcoal when I went out with the dog. A young girl was turning cartwheels on her lawn. I felt that I should warn her, upbraid her, tell her to go in, go in. We're losing the light and you'd best take flight for bad things happen at night, at night. But of course, I didn't.

Another girl, the same age, came down the sidewalk walking towards us. She was carrying a ball, a big orange ball. She held it in front of her, as if it were a baby she'd found and wasn't sure how to handle. She walked over the place where the hopscotch had been, she walked past me and the cartwheeling girl, she held out her ball without offering it and didn't look to the left or right, neither slowed nor quickened as she went on her mesmeric way, only walking, only walking, as if there were such a thing as safety in the world. As if she were following the sun.

a birthday letter

For Nora Beers Kelly, born June 21, 1995

dear Nora:

I'm writing this a few days before your first birthday. I'm writing this because I want to give you something I've made myself and sadly I have neither the tools nor the talent I'd need to hammer together a rocking horse, or a little red wagon, or any of the other more suitable remembrances a competent adult friend might think to give on so momentous an occasion. I wish it were otherwise. Unfortunately, I only use hammers for smashing ice and the sole contact I've had with a nail in the last 20 years was when I stepped on one. That forced me to learn how to spell "tetanus," which once proved useful for solving a crossword. Otherwise, I wouldn't recommend it. I'm writing this because words are pretty much my only hardware. Words and a charge card. I mention the charge card only because, years hence, I wouldn't want you to think that all I thought to give you on your first birthday was an 8 1/2-by-11-inch sheet of white bond. My dear! There are standards to uphold! Rest assured that you also received a drop-dead gorgeous, babe-o-rama ensemble from The Gap. But I wanted the thing I made to be something you could grow into. And it might be that in 12 or 15 years, when the coming millennium is no longer a novelty, you will read this. So, I am going to tell you what it was like to see you born.

That I was present at all is because your parents are my friends, and because I live with your godfather, who was in the delivery room as part of their support team. I am not someone who is constitutionally equipped to handle the viewing of so visceral a procedure as birth-giving. Just the thought of the pain and the necessary gore makes my blood rush to my toes, compels me to put my head between my knees. I had been happy to watch the outward evidence of your moonlike growth in utero, was happy to think about seeing you when the hard work was done and you were wiped down, swaddled up, and ready for public viewing. I was happy to wait at home for the phone call.

But as you were taking a very long time to elbow your way down the birth canal, and as I was growing bored, I went down to the hospital where I could at least watch your progress on a foetal heart monitor that was set up in the hall. I was minding my own business, studying the comforting "all's well" blip on the screen, listening for the telltale wail of a newborn. A nurse approached me. She said you were on the verge of arriving. She said that if I wanted to see the delivery, I should come in now. To this day, I'm not sure at whose behest this invitation was issued. To this day, I can't remember saying yes. To this day, I can't believe I saw it.

It was a crowded room. Your mother, your father, your godfather, your grandmother from Alaska, your grandparents from California, the doctor, the nurse, and what seemed to be half a dozen unassigned medical personnel were all in there gulping up the oxygen. The air was heavy with their collective concentration, thick with a kind of attenuated expectancy. Moving from the cool remove of the hallway and into that focussed heat was like stepping into a microclimate at the other end of the emotional register, like moving from temperate to tropical with the opening and closing of a door. It took me a few minutes to adjust to the change. I tried to steady myself in the moment by holding back, by looking around the room, by thinking that everyone who was waiting, watching, working was there because a woman had done this. I told myself that this very thing was happening in the birthing suite next door, in a hospital across town, that it was happening all over the planet. And then, every defence melted. Then I was wholly present in the room and it was the only place in the world and you were its only purpose.

I would never have thought that I'd feel pride in such a situation. Nevertheless, there it was, pride welling. I was proud of your father and godfather, who amazed me with their competence and calm, amazed me with knowing what to do, to say. I was incredibly proud of your mother, amazed by the intensity of her concentration, amazed that anyone could work that hard, that long, amazed by her buoyancy. I was proud of the community that had taken root in that room, proud that we were relative strangers, connected to each other and to all of history, to the past and the future, by this gruelling pushing, by this turning inside out. And I was proud of you as the top of your skull emerged and retreated, emerged and retreated, as the whole of the crown squeezed through, flesh out of flesh, and suddenly you were a face, and you opened your huge eyes and everyone in the room was astonished by how wide and beautiful they were, and then, in a second, there was all of you, and you were a girl, and your whole life was spreading in front of you, wide, in every direction, rich with possibility, with everything that is hard and beautiful. I heard the word "holy" in my head, and holy is what it was. I will never have the right words to say how lucky I was to have been there. How much I was blessed. Happy, happy birthday, Nora. Many, many more.

a book in the hand

Stéphane Mallarmé, the nineteenth-century French symbolist recently voted "Poet Most Likely to Be Mistaken for a Breakfast Condiment," wrote: «. . . *et l'hiver resterait la saison créatrice intellectuelle.»* I always find I share a great commonality of thought with Mallarmé, especially when it comes to his critical writings on Poe and his commonsensical approach to deficit reduction. However, I am particularly mindful of this, the most profound and pithy of his seasonal sentiments. As much for me as for Stéphane—more so, even, considering that he's dead and everything—winter will always be the season in which I undertake (and I use the word advisedly) what I blushingly refer to as my intellectual and creative work.

In this, I suspect, I am not alone. When I hear people speculating about why a country as sparsely populated as Canada should have produced such a vibrant squad of astoundingly good writers, I always want to timidly raise my hand and suggest that, like everything else, it all comes down to the weather. Given what most of us have to contend with between the Day of the Dead and Victoria Day, the prospect of lingering indoors, hovering over a heating vent and agonizing over the placement of a semicolon, becomes really, really attractive. It doesn't feel like a sacrifice, doesn't much require the imposition of some external discipline such as being shackled to the desk. No, you can keep your chains in the trunk of your Pinto where they might be useful, should you be foolish enough to venture out and find yourself stuck on an icy road. In short, it is no accident that only a single consonant distinguishes the words "writer" and "winter."

For the writer, winter is a time of growth and harvest, and summer is the time for sowing. Summer is the season for recharging the batteries, for replenishing the wellspring, for laying the table for the muse, for sterilizing the forceps used by literature's midwife. Or obstetrician. Legislation on this point varies from region to region across the country. While there is no guarantee that the hoped-for regeneration will take place, the surest way I know of facilitating such a fertilizing is through reading. Reading and writing are without doubt part of a continuum, and reading, even more than travel, is where writing begins.

All writers who share a language have the same tools at their disposal. They all use the same lexicon, they all explore the same themes, and the only way they can nudge themselves out of the vocational complacency that naturally settles on them as a consequence of spending so much time alone organizing sentences into paragraphs, into chapters, is to study how their colleagues make use of identical materials to achieve such startlingly different results. Reading can take on an edge that is both celebratory and competitive, and this (as Martha Stewart would say) is a good thing. Innovation, when it comes, is not born of isolation. It's only by observing another writer's craft, by taking note of how he handles the ins and outs of love or envy or longing; by admiring or looking askance at how she does it differently, does it better, or worse, that the reader finds the wherewithal to become a writer again, come the bleak midwinter.

This is not to say that writing is about imitation, although it can be that, but it is certainly about echo. Summer reading resonates in winter writing not through slavish parroting but in subtler ways. The discarding of old habits. A willingness to take more chances. A slight shift in the centre of gravity. This happens. It's an honourable and necessary part of the process. The same principle could be applied to painting, or to tennis, or to software engineering. It could be applied to cooking, come to that. You need someone else to come in and stir the pot for new flavours to emerge.

I don't mean to suggest that summer reading is a necessary chore or obligation, like detonating the weeds or getting a booster shot. It's a pleasure too, and as a pleasure it is qualitatively different from reading in the deepfreeze. When I have the chance to read in the winter, it's almost never with a plan in mind. I pick up whatever happens to be close to hand, whatever has been given to me, whatever has had a glowing review or appears on the best-seller list, or whatever I might have to read for work. In other words, I am getting a fix, feeding a habit, reacting rather than acting. In the winter, I am a passive reader. In the summer, round about the middle of June, I almost always set myself a project. Typically, this will have to do with filling some of the lacunae in my reading, and very often I will make my focus one author. Usually, though not always, I will set my sights on someone who's safely dead and out of the way so that I can get through the whole canon without worrying that he or she will sneak up behind me on an inside track and meet me at the finish line with something new.

It's shocking what and whom I've still to read, and someday, if you catch me in a confessional mood, I'll spill all the terrible beans. Three summers ago I finally had to look at myself in the mirror and admit that the only Jane Austen I'd ever managed was *Pride and Prejudice*, and that was under duress. So, I made my way through the others (well, most of the others, I didn't do *The Watsons*, even though I have some cousins who go by that name) and was powerfully glad I did. It didn't feel like work at all, and it also allowed me to be in fashion when she came into her own on both the small and big screens. Suddenly, everyone was talking about her. Not even the great Miss Jane was immune to the prevailing belief that a book is not sufficient unto itself and that it only achieves its apotheosis when it becomes a movie or a miniseries.

Two summers ago I turned 40, and was so traumatized by the event that I read nothing but self-help books, which didn't work, as anyone who knows me will quickly attest. This past summer I decided to give myself heart and soul to Iris Murdoch. I read *The Flight from the Enchanter, A Fairly Honourable Defeat,* and *The Sea, the Sea,* and was halfway through *The Philosopher's Pupil* when I finally had to admit that I just didn't like Iris Murdoch, didn't like her nasty characters and their hateful ways, and didn't want to ruin my summer with them. I turned to Mary Wesley instead, and was much, much happier. Of course, when I learned that Iris Murdoch was ill and would probably never write again, I was full of a kind of stupid remorse. Perhaps she is not the sort of writer who should be taken in in one fell swoop. This summer, perhaps I will try to make it up to her.

If I had to point to one aspect of reading that pleases me above all others, I would say that what I like best is that it is a private affair. Sometimes we want to shut out even our nearest and dearest, and there is no better way to do that than with a book. The only creature who can safely violate the sacred space between this reader and the page is my cat, when she is in a lap-dancing mood. Otherwise, like Garbo, *I vant to be alone.* I hate reading out loud to one other person, and can't abide being read to. I am a control freak in this regard and want to observe the narrative as it is played out in the theatre of my own imagining.

When we think of summertime reading, however, there is almost always an aberrant public dimension that comes into play. This has to do with the idea of reading outdoors, in company, and almost always on the beach. I am amazed that so many people manage this so successfully, or at least so willingly, and that they are able to neutralize or ignore the many impediments to reading that are part and parcel of *la plage*. (The phonetic connection between *"plage"* and "plague," especially in a bilingual country, is no more random than that between "writer" and "winter.") All the elements that make the beach attractive to people who like the beach—sun, sand, water, the smell of roasting human flesh, the cloying waft of oil and lotion, the spectacle of buffed young people sporting about on the shore, and so on—are anathema to anyone who wants to enjoy the quiet communion that is reading. There are so many distractions, so many annoyances. Loud music, grains in the eye, glare on the page, head injuries incurred by vociferously spiked volleyballs, the imminence of melanoma: all these siphon attention away from the matter at hand, bibliographically speaking, and nourish the idea that summer, above all else, is a time to equate recreation with vacuity.

Not that I'm immune to such tactics of sunny suasion. Oh, no. I'm not some Mr. High and Mighty squinting out from between the slats of his venetian blinds, high up in some ivory tower; not some tightlipped priss sneering at the wasteful fools who frolic below. Nosirree Bob! Like everyone else, I start out every summer imagining that my life will resemble a beer commercial. Like everyone else, I'll make a trip to the beach from time to time, and always with book in hand. Often, just around this time of year, I will wend my way out to the University of British Columbia and slip-slide down the sandy, eroding cliffs to Wreck Beach. There, I will doff my duds and splay upon a log, just me, my chosen tome, and the bookmark God gave me. Girded only by virtue, I'll read, trying not to be distracted by the vendors selling frozen daiquiris, by the pot peddlers, by the waft of sewage coming off the inlet. I'll apply myself as diligently as I can to the page, averting my gaze from the various views. Call me a cockeyed optimist, but every year I think I'll be able to bring this off. And every year I wind up giving in, closing my book, and joining in the passing parade. Another chance to read, shot to hell! Oh, how my writing to come will suffer for this! Oh, well. There are times when the mind just can't be allowed to win, and that's not a bad lesson to learn, even in middle age. If you're down at Wreck, I'll be easy to spot. Look for the pasty guy with the daiquiri, and a copy of *The Philosopher's Pupil* under his arm. Come say howdy. We can talk about how much we're looking forward to the winter.

my most memorable field trip experience

Composition assignment for English 201, section B. Instructor: Ms. F. Kooner

Last week's Supreme Court decision that B.C. school boards may no longer levy charges on students for classroom materials and sundry extras may result in certain cancellations, such as field trips. Write about your most memorable field trip experience. 100 words. Due tomorrow by 3:00 p.m. No excuses. You will be graded. This assignment will count for 10% of your final mark.

1. "My Most Memorable Field Trip Experience" by Jamie Botnarchuck. A story in 100 words. I was so very happy on that very beautiful Monday morning in the spring, when the grass was very green, the sky was very blue, and everyone in New Age Studies crowded into the very yellow school bus. I sat beside Tiffany, who was sitting in front of Brie, who was sitting with Jason because they'd just started going out, and then we all went off on our field trip to the colonic irrigationist. It was very, very interesting. I will never, never forget it. Never. Word count: 100.

2. "My Most Memorable Field Trip Experience" by Andrew Rigby. A story in 100 words. Last February, the Future Physician's Club went to watch an autopsy. It was a very memorable afternoon. The corpse was none other than Mr. Schaefer, my English teacher from September 1995 through February 1996. It was fascinating to hear the pathologist detail the specifics of the dreadful injuries that led to Mr. Schaefer's untimely death. I felt badly, even though he gave me a C– on an assignment, which is not a pre-med admissions kind of mark. As everyone should know. Oh, well. That's all! Word count: 100.

3. "An Unforgettable Field Trip." A 100-word essay by Amabile Fernspray. My soul was scorched, as if by a blast of lightning from the sceptre of Zeus himself. My soul trembled, as if it were a baby bird fallen early from the nest. My soul was taut as a too-tight fiddle string, my soul was a refrigerator with a burned-out bulb, my soul was an uncleaned lint trap, my soul was a hotel shower with someone else's curly hair on the tile. All this was my soul when Jason sat beside Brie on the way to the colonic irrigationist. Word count: 100.

4. "Our Class Trip to the Abattoir" by Ulysses Sisson. Mostly I guess the reason I will never forget the trip we made to the abattoir was because I'd understood we were going on an "abbey tour," which I thought would be fun because I played Rolfe in our production of *The Sound of Music* last year, as you must remember, it's a small part but everyone agreed that I was memorable, especially my singing of "You Are Sixteen" and the way I looked in those shorts, but it just turned out to be pigs on hooks and some free sausage. Word count: 100.

5. "A Field Trip I Will Never Forget, As Long As I Live" by Jackileen Lindner. I glanced up from my book, *This Savage Longing*, and saw the unmistakable glower of hatred on her face. Her eyes were guttering coals. Her young breasts heaved. Her lips were a grim, ochre gash. She was a woman scorned, there could be no question. She had the look of one who craved revenge like a vampire craves blood. I will never forget that look, nor the way she shuddered when the bus driver announced, "Okay, everyone! We're here! All out for the colonic irrigationist!" Word count: 100.

6. "My Most Memorable Field Trip" by Courtney Leung, a composition for Ms. Kooner in exactly 100 words, not one more and not one less, including the title. I was looking forward to our trip to the abattoir, because I had heard they give you free sausage, which is my favourite meat. Imagine how disappointed I was when it turned out that we were going on an "ABBA Tour." What good will the lyrics to "Fernando" be to me in my chosen profession of

butchering? It would have been much more beneficial to me to learn "The Wiener Takes It All." Word count: 100.

7. "An Unforgettable Field Trip, Like, Totally" by Brie Feather-stone. It was like, you know, not my fault that Jason decided he liked me better than he liked her. Like, you know, who can blame him? I mean, like, Amabile, fix your hair, chick, you'll stand a chance. So like, there we were in this place, and it was like gross, with all these tubes and charts, like, and Jason—he is totally cool—was whispering "a butt tour" and this geek asked for a volunteer, and Amabile said, "Jason is full of shit." She is a bitch. Really. I mean, like, totally. Word count: 100.

8. "A Memorable Field Trip" by Patrick Semple. My most memo-rable field trip was to Rome with Italian 101. We went there last summer. We stayed in a very nice hotel. The weather was very warm. The food was very good. There was a nice pool. One day in the pool I met the Pope and the College of Cardinals. They leave their robes and rings on, even when they swim. We talked for a long time about papal infallibility. I gave him some advice on deal-ing with schismatics. Then the Pope made me a bishop. He was nice. The end. Word count: 100.

9. "The Field Trip That Changed My Life" by Jason Mohr. "Lie still," said the colonic irrigationist, "I'll give her some juice." He turned the faucet. I felt the warm gush. The phone rang in the other room. "Excuse me," he said, "I'll be just a moment. Don't touch anything!" No sooner had he left the room than Amabile leapt for-ward. She grabbed the faucet. She cranked it hard. I hardly knew what hit me! The scales washed from my eyes. I saw I'd been blind. This was true love. Explosive. Wet. We belong together. And I will never forget it. Word count: 100.

livid pink

A Tragedy in Verse, Written under the Influence of Paint Chips.
The Author Acknowledges His Indebtedness to Home Hardware.

She met him in the hardware
store—it was a *Rosy Day*,
He felt a *Warm Glow* dawning when he saw her glance his way.
His eyes were bright as *Amethyst*, her hair the hue of *Toast*,
And each could tell that *Destiny* had lashed them to his post.

The *Winter Solstice* long was passed. The heady *Breath of Spring*
Was like a *Dress Rehearsal* for the songs that summer sings:
A spritely *Opera Prelude* that forebodes the fierce *Monsoon*,
When morning's *Minuet* achieves *Blue Rhapsody* by noon.

He said, "My name's *Tiberius*. Like you, I'm buying paint.
Your colour is *Alluring*, while my *Bristol*'s rather quaint.
Perhaps you'd like to mix our shades, make *Bridal Party* blush?
And I'll provide the *Pollen* if you'll just provide the brush."

She was a *Pink Romantic* and *Paloma* was her name,
She had an *Old World* background and she understood his
        game.
In *Dauphin* and in *Baghdad* she'd been told she was a dish.
She was no *Prima Donna*, but she always got *Her Wish*.

She said, "Why, it's been ages since I had a *Stormy Night*.
I *Fathom* that you like me, since your jeans are rather tight.
We'll make a sweet *Sensation*, but let's first go have a nosh,
And for dessert we'll pressure-cook your precious *Hopi Squash*."

He clicked his heels, his *Star Blue* eyes shone like a *Lightning Bug*.
He'd shortly lay his *Cockleshell* inside her wicker trug.
Oh, this was no *Ice Folly*, these were *Cupid*'s halcyon days!
He felt his *Cornbread* rising as he bought his *Mystic Maize*.

A *Botticelli* Venus, she had style and great *Finesse*.
Her hair was like *Spun Gold*; of *Spanish Leather* was her dress.
His heart was full of *Passion*, and it seemed both plain and clear
They'd end the night by swinging from a well-hung *Chandelier*.

They found a *Stellar* restaurant, and they sat there, quite
enthralled.
They ate *Vanilla Custard* and a plate of *Melon Balls*.
Their wine had floral overtones: "*Lobelia*, I think,"
He said while in the *Brick Dust* west the sun commenced to sink.

He called her *Yellow Duchess* while her fingertips he kissed,
He whispered "*Mi piace*" through a faux *Italian Mist*.
He whispered "Be my *Fuchsia Rose*," which some would find too
much,
But he could push love's envelope, he had the *Midas Touch*.

He said, "Let's watch the *Moon Mystique*, and walk along the
beach."
She said, "But first let's have dessert. Let's order *Serene Peach*."
"An *Inspiration*!" he replied, in well-worn lover's code.
"*Visionary*! And what's more, let's have it *A La Mode*!"

In truth, he'd eaten too much fruit. Like some *Nocturnal Sea*
His guts began a tidal shift. "*Mademoiselle*," said he,
"*Excusez-moi*!" All *Banner Red*, intestines primed to toss,
He fled the room. She ordered up more hot *Spiced Applesauce*.

An hour later he returned, his visage *Spanish Blue*,
To find his *Wild Carnation* gone. She'd left a note: "We're
through!
Our *Elegant Evening*'s over, and the point is far from moot:
I won't go make a *Daisy Chain* if you can't hold your fruit.

"Your *Myth* has been exploded, so I'm telling you, we're done.
I've run off with the waiter to the land of *Midnight Sun*.
You'll have to pet your *Chipmunk* by yourself, I'm on the lam:
As *Scarlett O'Hara* often heard, I just don't give a damn!"

And so his night of *Gaiety* was snuffed out in a trice.
His torrid *Yellow Warbler* now was shrunken, cold as ice.
His *Delicate Bloom* had ditched him, had not deigned to share
    his bed.
She'd donned her little *Toe Shoes*, through the *Distance* now she fled.

She craved her *Independence*. *Freedom* had its *Golden Gleam*.
And he was left to *Stargaze* after what things might have been.
Love's radiant *Corona* with a *Blue Shade* brush was tarred,
Its *Pink Aurora* faded, and the *August Sun* rose *Noir*.

treadmill

"**T**oo bad," said my father when I came through the door, "that you weren't here yesterday. You could have watched me sand your teeth marks from the window ledge."

My parents live in Winnipeg and I hadn't seen them in over a year. Dad is a master of the odd opening gambit.

"Teeth marks?" I asked, setting down my valise. This was a bit of family lore I'd never heard before.

"You were so sweet," said my mother. I could tell she was itching to get her hands on my jeans so she could launder them and iron in razor-sharp creases. "You used to haul yourself up to the kitchen window, hang onto the frame, look out at the back yard, and have a good old chew."

"When I was teething?"

I thought the question was rhetorical.

"Oh, no! You had all your teeth. I think you just liked the taste of the wood. We used to call you our little beaver. So cute!"

I ran my hand over the smooth surface of the ledge from which my dental traces had been so recently expunged. I felt a small and unreasonable sadness at this cavalier erasure of the evidence that once I passed this way. You can go home again, easily enough. But as time goes by, you just can't count on finding the same old souvenirs.

"Well, after all," I chided myself as I hiked my baggage up the stairs, "it's their house, not a sacred reliquary. Why shouldn't they devote their declining years to removing blemishes from around the windows?"

Cleaving to a perspective as tempered and as grownup as this is not easy when you're back under the roof that sheltered your childhood. When I opened the door to my old room, I came within a hair's-breadth of giving in to a full-scale pout. Nothing was the same! What was mine was gone. The familiar crannies and corners were jammed with alien stuff.

"Different, isn't it?" said my father, who had followed me up. "We didn't know where else to put the old furniture when we remodelled. And there was so much of it that I hardly had room for the walking machine your mother gave me for Christmas. It's quite the gizmo. I'll show you how it works."

I sank into the practised embrace of a well-worn Danish modern couch, while he mounted and fired up the treadmill, a DP Transport LP 6200. "On a good day," he shouted over the rumble of its guts, "I'll do three miles! And you can adjust the speed!" He flicked a switch. His feet moved faster. The machine sounded like a thousand rodents gnawing a thousand window ledges.

What on earth had come over him? For years, he seemed content to live the sedentary life, much like the one I myself enjoy. He was my example. When friends would mock my days of constructive sloth, I would fall back on genetics to explain it all. My father's few recreations were mild and domestic. Running, race walking, aerobics, roller blading: these were all fads or ideas whose seductive whisperings had never snagged or engaged him. I watched other seniors enter marathons and take up power lifting, and wished them well. But my father's unwavering lack of interest in such activities was an inspiration to me. He was a rock of stability in an all too protean world. He was impervious to fashion. Now this! This walking machine was the slippery slope of the thin edge of the wedge! What would it be in another year? Spandex shorts and a step class at the Y?

"Come take a look!" he shouted.

The DP Transport LP 6200 comes equipped with a talented gauge called the "Bionix Multiple Display." He pointed at it with a loopy kind of pride. On it, I could read a statistical measure of his physical worth: speed, distance, time, calories expended, pulse.

I stood watching the changing numbers make visible some of the truths of my father's secret body. I stood in his heat, getting used to the idea that there was much he hadn't told me and much he had yet to tell. His fast-moving feet were taking him precisely nowhere, but I felt the dawning of the certainty it wouldn't be that way for long.

dogwood

The tree my father turned into a dog was an oak, which was a commonplace tree on Hart Avenue. But the species chosen by the landscape architect who had designed our subdivision never achieved the glory implicit in that name. Oak: the many-ringed, thick-trunked, and lordly trees of Sherwood, O dark and brooding sacred gathering place of the Druids. This was not for Hart Avenue. Ours were gaunt and craggy oaks that grew tall but not wide, trees whose rasping bark was flecked by a feathery, orange moss.

They weren't very useful trees. Their branches would never be sufficiently sturdy nor appropriately spaced to accommodate a tree house. They provided only inconsequential shade from the summer sun: perhaps enough to shelter a very thin child and a very small lemonade stand, or for a dog to find some sort of tongue-lolling comfort during the hottest part of the day. In the fall the oaks up and down the street all shed a quantity of brown leaves that seemed wholly disproportionate to the degree of protection they had afforded during their greener lifetimes. The leaves were a chore-making annoyance. At the same time, though, a feeling of happy community fell over Hart Avenue on that Saturday morning late in September when, through instinct, everyone went to the basement or backyard shed and excavated the rake. This was in the days before the advent of green plastic garbage bags, before city officials in a magnanimous show of concern for our pulmonary well-being forbade the burning of leaves. This was well before Les Thornton next door died of the hiccups, before baby Paul across the street traded in his Beverly Hillbillies lunchbucket for an electric guitar and a Mohawk. This was before Mrs. Wingrave decided that seventy-three was not too old to learn the harmonica and did, and then one summer evening after one too many gin and tonics stood at the top of her steps playing "Old Folks at Home" with nothing on, and someone called the police and after that she went away to live with her daughter.

The raking of leaves always took longer than was strictly necessary. A one-hour sweep-up would have been sufficient for their simple gathering, but more time was needed to explore their possibilities. Leaves could be picked up and thrown, leaves could be piled and then jumped in, again and again, until parental tempers ran thin and the dross of the oaks was gathered into cardboard boxes and taken to backyard incinerators to be turned into gold.

The oaks also produced a goodly quantity of acorns. Some acorns were conscientiously left behind for the squirrels. Many would be gathered up with the leaves as bonfire food. They made satisfying popping sounds in the flames. Myths had grown up around the acorns. One was said to have exploded in a fire a few streets over and the flying shell blinded someone. Acorns were thought to be poisonous to humans, just like the mysterious purple berries that grew on the nameless shrubs everyone had planted to mask the jutting hot-air vents from their dryers. Every year, as a kind of rite of passage, a few of the bigger boys, who only the year before stood back away from the fire for fear of wearing an eye patch for the rest of their days, would peel back the shell from the acorn and eat the rosy-veined, peach-coloured meat. When immediate death did not result from this daring, some other danger would be found.

"Holy geez, didja see the size of the worm hangin' outta that one that Kenny ate? Dintcha see it, Kenny? It was hardly that big! I know a kid who ate a worm like that once and a few nights later he woke up 'cause he couldn't breathe 'cause the worm had crawled up from his stomach and into his nose."

Those were hazy afternoons on Hart Avenue. The leaves turned into aromatic ghosts. Women blew smoke rings and waved to each other from doorways. Men leaned on their rakes and addressed laconic remarks to their neighbours, grunt-like utterances issued from behind pipestem-clenching teeth. The younger children, those who wouldn't yet dare to swallow an acorn, tugged at their fathers' pant legs, begging for an acorn pipe. These were crafted by lopping

the top off an acorn with a pen knife, cutting out the meat and pre-
serving the shell. When a small twig was inserted into the bottom
of the bowl as a stem, the result was a dandy pipe.

My father carved the best acorn pipes on Hart Avenue, a fact
acknowledged even by the conceited Lorelei who lived down the
street. Other fathers, well-meaning but maladroit, turned out a
product that was scarcely a notch above what had been given them
by nature. My father made art. He would scrape away the nut so
carefully and thoroughly that only a porcelain-thin and eggshell-
light skin remained. Working quickly and delicately, he would
score the casing so that the bowl was rough textured, like a corn-
cob pipe. Perhaps he would engrave a small heart or a diamond or
a four-leaf clover on it. "It's just whittling," he would say dismis-
sively when he handed us the finished pipe.

My father, a banker, had always "just whittled." He carved a
seagull perched on a rock, its wide wings spread, its beak clamped
onto a fish. He carved a heron, spindly legged against rushes. He
carved an Indian head from a photograph by Edward Curtis. Birds
or Indians, he always worked from photographs. The time he
turned the oak into a dog was the only time he ever worked from
life. The dog was Mitchell, our mongrel, who looked as much like
a springer spaniel as he looked like anything. My father turned him
into oak at the tag end of the dog's life, when Mitchell was half
blind and too tired out to be anything but a complacent model. In
palmier days, when he had been a thin-blooded, handsome dog
around town, Mitch had led a colourful life. He had bitten both
the postman and our minister. He was a playboy who carried on
his romantic intrigues in the schoolyard. I never knew when I
might look from my classroom window and see him frolicking dis-
gracefully with Muffin, with Sheba, and, once, with Rinty.

"Isn't Rinty a boy dog?" I asked my mother that day after
school.

"I believe so," she answered. "Why?"

"No reason."

For where would I find the words to tell her what I had seen?

The oak that became Mitchell was one of two in our front yard.
It had become diseased and needed to be removed. The operation
left behind a stump that stood about eight feet tall. It was
unsightly, and the sensible thing would have been to remove it alto-

gether, and plant in its stead a silver maple, which would have been patriotic; or a lilac, which would have been fragrant; or an elm, which would have been shortsighted, given the Dutch elm blight that was soon to sneak onto Hart Avenue.

But my father saw with the presumptive eye of the sculptor. It was his small vanity to believe that he could see into the heart of wood and find revealed there the true nature and ambitions of insentient matter. For him, wood was never sufficient unto itself. It was a dark prison where some hidden form lay in bondage. His was the mission of the liberator, and through the tightly circled rings of the stump of the oak he saw Mitchell struggling to be free.

The oak came down in the spring, and all that summer— Mitchell's last dog days—my father worked. He stripped off the bark from the corpsey trunk, turning it into a column, a pedestal on which Mitchell would perch for something like eternity. Mitchell himself, antique and doddering, destined in the winter to be dispatched to meet his maker through the chemical mercies of the veterinarian, was insensible to his immortalization. He spent that whole season of his sculpting in a happy green stupor on the grass, enjoying whatever smells came his way, but too wise and exhausted to do anything about them. The new generation of squirrels—who must certainly have heard tales of the fearsome beast from their beleaguered parents—were given every reason to wonder at the caveats of their elders. It was not true that this dog would chase them mercilessly and bark threats as they ran along the telephone wires. No, they could frolic undisturbed under his very nose if they cared to. And they did. The cat across the street, whose life he had made a misery for a dozen years, came to understand that her old foe was a menace no longer. Time had been kinder to her, a fact she never tired of flaunting by stalking birds in plain view of God and Mitchell, neither of whom thought it worth the trouble to strike her down. Muffin, Sheba, and Rinty had died or left Hart Avenue years before, but had one of them somehow appeared and tried to entice Mitchell back to the schoolyard with erotic blandishments, he would have regarded them with rheumy eyes, grinned a doggy grin of fond recall, and drifted back to sleep.

"Whatcha up to, Stan?" asked the neighbours as my father stood on his stepladder, chisel in one hand and mallet in the other.

"Whittling. Just whittling."

"Well, what's it going to be, Stan? Totem pole or something?"
"Nope. Dog."
"Oh. That'll be nice then, won't it. Good luck, Stan."

The stump of the oak measured about 30 inches in diameter. Given these dimensions, it would have been impossible to carve the dog as he was, all placid and supine. Both the width of the tree and my father's sense of artistic purpose dictated that Mitchell's permanent posture should be more dignified. Bit by bit, chips of the stump were knocked away to reveal a sitting dog, his back straight, his profile patrician, his spaniel ears long and silky, his waistcoat feathered.

"Why, that's Mitchell. It certainly is," exclaimed Mrs. Woolman, whose cancer was still only a small twinge, but who would not see another spring.

"What a talent you have, Stan," said the newly widowed Mrs. Thornton, who was soon to move to Calgary.

What the neighbours said privately, I have no idea. Perhaps it did not strike them as unusual or eccentric that a man would carve a dog out of a tree in the front yard. Perhaps they didn't mind that the traffic picked up on quiet Hart Avenue as word of the dog carver got out and people drove by in the evening to study the sculptor's progress. Perhaps they were genuinely delighted to learn of my father's talents. Certainly they were surprised. He had always kept his whittling a private business, apart from the acorn pipes. By the time he turned the oak into a dog, our childish delight at these had been supplanted by more grownup enthusiasms.

Looking back, I'm surprised that my father wasn't nonplussed by the attention he received that summer. He was then, and still is, a solitary and undemonstrative sort. Perhaps, in his way, he was really making a public statement. Not a boast, but a simple declaration. "Look. You think I am a man who works in a bank, a pleasant man of few words. But here is what I truly am, a man who sees into the heart of wood."

The summer passed, the chisel chipped, and by the time the remaining oaks had spilled their leaves, both Mitchells were almost done. Early in the winter, my father picked up the dog from the slippery kitchen linoleum where Mitchell had fallen one too many times, and carried him out past his oaken likeness to the car. When my father came home, he phoned in sick to work, made some tea, and sat all day quietly in his chair. He didn't carve anything all the rest of that season. In January, when the prairie weather was bitter, he put a woollen toque on the wooden dog. In the spring he found an eagle imprisoned in a block of walnut, and went back to whittling.

what a good girl

my fat dog, Smoke, has been so successful in her recent weight-loss program that powerful Hollywood interests have been hounding her, so to speak, to star in one of those fitness videos celebrities are forever cranking out. She spends hour after hour meeting with moguls in stretch limos. She comes home with Perrier on her breath and a gleam in her eye. This is Smoke's gravy train, and she knows it.

Yesterday, I managed to pry her away from her cellular long enough to ask if she would allow me to have some kind of involvement in the project, perhaps as the writer. Her response was that if I wanted to submit a "treatment," as they say in the biz, she'd give it due consideration, along with the five or six dozen others that have already made their way over her transom. She warned me, however, that when it came to business matters she would prove hardheaded, and not be swayed by the fact that it was I who only two months ago shelled out almost 500 bucks so that she could have a disfiguring polyp removed from her otherwise blameless toe.

I think my chances of making my way to the top of the slush pile are minimal, at best. Nonetheless, here is my game plan for *What a Good Girl: Smoke's Two-Month One-Pound Weight-Loss Program*.

Fade in on Smoke, reclining at home. She is wearing fur and looks very alluring. Against a backwash of soft New Age music, a soothing voice (Meryl Streep?) provides the narrative buttressing for the visuals.

Narrator: Welcome to Smoke's World of Fitness. It's not just an exercise program! It's a whole new lifestyle that will allow you to lose up to one pound in two months without need of dieting or giving up the foods you love! All you need to do is to follow this straightforward exercise regime and regularly repeat Smoke's Weight-Loss Affirmation: "Good girl! Good girl!" Ready? Let's go.

Begin your daily workout with these warm-up exercises. Follow along as Smoke shows you how. Lie on your back on the chesterfield, with your four limbs splayed toward each of the cardinal points. Good girl! Maintain this position for three or four hours— or more, if it feels comfortable—pausing every fifteen minutes or so to shed. Good girl! End this section of the program with a visualization. You are in the park. You see a squirrel. You chase it! Good girl! Now relax, with your four limbs splayed.

These next exercises are for flexibility. Rise, stretch, and roll from the couch. Assume a lying position. Now, extend your head toward your nether parts and lick them vigorously. Good girl! Rise and stretch. Now, amble to the kitchen and sit beneath the cookie jar and stretch your neck. Really stretch it! Good girl! Wag your tail. Shake a paw. Now—jump into the air and take that cookie! Chew! And swallow! And chew! And swallow! Good girl!

(The music gets funky, and the narrator picks up the tempo.)

Narrator: Grab a partner and get ready for Smoke's Cardio Workout! Ready to go for a walk? Good girl! Jump up and down on the hardwood! Jump until you scratch the heck out of it! Run around in circles while your partner tries to put you on your leash! That's good exercise for both of you. Now, bolt down the stairs. Run as fast as you can until the leash pulls you up short! Smoke does this day after day and never gets tired of it! Ready to try it? Good girl! Run! Jerk back! Run! Jerk back! That's excellent. If you're comfortable with that, move on to the most challenging aspect of Smoke's workout: Sniff and Lunge. Ready? Begin! Lunge! Lunge! Sniff! Lunge! Lunge! Sniff! Again! Again! Now poo, poo, poo! Good girl! Wait till your partner leans over with his bag! Now lunge! Lunge! Lunge! Keep it up till you get home. Eat three biscuits.

What a good girl! Now you're ready for Smoke's Cool Down. Lie on your back on the chesterfield with your four limbs splayed . . .

I'm onto something. I can feel it in my bones. Now, if I can only keep Smoke from returning those calls from Paula Abdul . . .

chain of events

One thing leads to another. For instance, I have this cat I named Kali, after the Hindu Goddess of destruction. She feels she has a reputation to uphold. She is also unaccountably partial to dog biscuits. The other day I left an unopened box of Milkbones atop the fridge. Acting either as her own agent, or with the encouragement of the dog, she strapped on her crampons, scaled the icebox, and shoved the box to the kitchen floor.

I wasn't there to see this happen, but I interpreted the chain of events from the dog-toothed remnants of packaging, the cat's sly smirk, and the dog's gourdlike belly. Puppy and kitty worked through those bickies at a ratio of 40 to 1, I figure.

One thing leads to another. Round about 2:00 a.m. I was out with Smoke, whose gastrointestinal situation had turned fitful. In our neighbourhood, at that time of the morning, the sidewalks are lousy with urban-adapted fauna, most especially skunks. Though I admire these cunningly decorated and well-armed creatures, I feel a tad edgy around them, particularly with a dog who is long on enthusiasm but, frankly, just a few quarters short of a roll. However, on this excursion, we met a skunk who filled me with nothing so much as a deep serenity. She was lying statuelike on the boulevard, her little forepaws curled catlike beneath her chest. She seemed to be meditating. It was very calming. Even Smoke, normally agitated around these creatures, showed no urge to lunge but seemed content to sit quietly and reflect on her sins. It was a very still moment.

One thing leads to another. As we lingered, mesmerized by this unlikely hypnotist, my brain was inhabited by lines of a Robert Lowell poem, "Skunk Hour." He writes of "skunks that search / In the moonlight for a bite to eat / They march on their soles up Main Street." I recollected that he dedicated this to Elizabeth Bishop, and that she in turn had inscribed to him her poem "Armadillo." It's set in Brazil, where she spent much of her adult life, and it describes a festival night's fire balloons. "Once up against the sky / It's hard to tell them from the stars / Planets that is: the tinted ones / Venus going down, or Mars / Or the pale green one."

I am a know-nothing about astronomy. I have a faint idea that Venus is visible in the late dusky air around this time of summer, and Mars is up there somewhere too, a little red around the edges. With Elizabeth Bishop echoing in my nearly empty head, I stared up at the heavily punctuated sky, trying to discern which might be Venus, which might be Mars. Were they there? Or was it past their bedtime? I wondered too, with a twinge of concern, about poor old Jupiter, which is due to be bombarded by the sizeable shards of a comet it made the mistake of inviting into its orbit. The relationship was too much for the comet to bear. That's what happens when you aspire to intimacy in the nineties.

This planetary pelting is a rare event, and astronomers are over the moon about the chance to study the tragic end days of Shoemaker-Levy 9—for that is the comet's cumbersome name. Of course there's been much speculation on the part of idle millenarians as to whether or not the same thing might happen to Earth one day, and even about the off chance that the bombarding of Jupiter by speedball space debris might set in motion a chain of events that will bring the curtain down on life as we know it. One thing leads to another, after all.

"What do you think, skunk?" I asked, my head still tilted toward the night sky. But when I looked down for her answer, I found she had toddled away. Venus and Mars, I suspect, had done the same. Who did they leave behind? Me. The dog. A tremulous Jupiter. And a vast array of stars, strung across the heavens like charms on a bracelet. They beamed their thousand-year-old light onto this proud and wobbling accident of a planet where these days Kali is queen, and where one thing leads inevitably to another, but where unsought moments of peace still unravel, and even the worst that we can imagine is never as big or as bad as it seems.

dog days

These are the dog days, which is one of the reasons I'm thinking about dogs, especially my dog, Smoke. I'm thinking about Smoke because the story of her life is as shaggy as they make 'em, and she needs a smart bob in the worst possible way, and she has been waiting for three weeks for an appointment at her beauty parlour of choice, which seems unfair as she is an old dog now and finds the heat more punishing than once she did. And she lies in the yard, a fat dog in thin shade, and her tongue lolls and she sweats in that special way that dogs sweat, drop by drop onto the browning grass. So, I'm thinking about dogs because these are dog days and also because it's getting to that time of year when fleas both demonstrate their easy fecundity and lay their vacation plans. Many, many of them love to travel to the land of Smoke, to experience the sweet, warm, nourishing climate of her underbelly, which is legendary for its frequent, fragrant winds, and from which base they can make many interesting side trips into my carpet pile and upholstery and bedding. So, I'm thinking about dogs because these are dog days and because the fleas are packing their bags, and also because I am experiencing what I take to be symptoms of the male change of life. Most of the nasty catalogue— career anxiety, troublesome loin-based longings, insecurity about the future of my teeth—I have been schooled to expect and can handle with something like wry insouciance. What I absolutely cannot accommodate, however, and what I absolutely cannot shake, is this intractable urge to buy a cherry-coloured pickup truck.

Let us set dogs to one side for just a moment, and consider why such an urge—this aberrant thirst that only a vehicle can slake— should come to the fore in the menopausal male. It is a well-docu-mented phenomenon. My own father, when he was about the age I am now, traded in his reliable Chrysler for a Volkswagen van. Lord knows why. He was too Protestant by half not to have his good reasons for making such a swap, but the truth was that it was neither a practical nor a necessary choice. The truth was that it was nothing more than some whim forced on him by the shifting cur-rents of one lobe or other. The truth was that he fancied the way he'd look behind the wheel, that he lived with this imagining day by day, and that finally he had no choice but to give in. There's ample anecdotal evidence to suggest that this condition is wide-spread. This city's arteries are plugged with middle-aged guys who are piloting sporty, shiny, expensive dickmobiles up and down the thoroughfares in a last-ditch effort to attract some young and fertile thing to whom they can disseminate their wobbly seed. It's as inevitable as it is risible. How long has it been going on? Forever, I suppose. I can't imagine that such a mode of behaviour settled on us with the dawning of the automotive age. Biology adapts itself to technology, and you can bet that in years gone by men in their forties were spending extravagant sums on an inappropriate coach and four, or chariot, or stone wheel, or what have you, and comporting themselves in the very same way.

So, I'm thinking about dogs because my own small brain is adjusting its chemistry and I can see myself so damn clearly, looking so damn fine, behind the wheel of my cherry pickup truck, a cute little one, compact and tight and neat, unsullied by evidence of agriculture, innocent of manure, and there's never once been a bale of straw or hay or oats or whatever the hell it is you wrap into bales slung into the back. I'm riding in the cab, high up but not too high, in a red plaid shirt but neatly pressed, and the window is rolled down, and there's country music, but not too loud, and not too country, not Garth Brooks but Mary Chapin Carpenter, only the slow sad songs. And look! There's Smoke! She's in the back, in the open, where the bales are meant to go, and she's standing up and looking out, she's taking in the passing scene, and she's shaggy but not hot, the scented wind keeps her both cool and interested, and she's struck with that blissful look that only belongs to dogs who get to ride in the back of a cherry pickup truck, and the world is her oyster, and we're not going anywhere in particular, Smoke and me and Mary Chapin Carpenter, no, we've got no place in mind, we're just cruising, cruising, cruising.

And I'm thinking about dogs because a friend just called to tell me about a three-legged puppy who needs a good home, and I'm thinking about Smoke, who doesn't have many more summers left to her, and I'm looking at my own life and thinking that I have time enough left for maybe two more dogs, no more than three, and I feel like a traitor, thinking already about old Smoke's replacement, but this could be opportunity knocking and it's a fact that I've always liked tripods and I could name him Triumph and what if I just said yes and wouldn't we be a sight, old shaggy Smoke and three-legged Triumph and me in our pickup—cherry, no other colour will do—just driving along the Kingsway for no good reason other than that it's the Kingsway, and we have a hankering to hear *Stones in the Road*, that it's the summer, that these are dog days, that we are growing older, that we are happy, that we are happy, that we are happy.

earthquake readiness: 2

There's this fellow I know from the boulevard who's addicted to prophecy. He seeks out psychics, wherever they might be. He visits them in restaurants. He sees them in their homes. He calls them at 1-900 numbers and hears their astonishing news on the phone.

When our paths crossed a few Saturdays back, round about midnight, he reported that three of his occult consultants had independently foreseen how the Mother of All Earthquakes would rumble through the neighbourhood at 6:30 on the following Sunday morning! In less than seven hours!

I have learned two important lessons in my life. One is: never feed the dog pickled beets, even though they are her favourite food and she begs for them very convincingly. The other is: always respect unanimity of opinion. So rather than discount these ravings, I pitched my tent in the camp of the believers.

Once, in a fit of uncharacteristic conscientiousness, I secured a "Surviving the Big One" pamphlet. It was full of good counsel about minimizing the perils and inconvenience of living in rubble. What to do. Where to stand. What to have on hand. And so on. I filed this useful document in a secure, earthquake-proof place, so of course I long ago lost track of it. I vaguely recalled advice about avoiding fallen power lines, turning off the gas, and eating tinned food until help arrived; although some of this may have come from literature on prospering during a nuclear attack. The tinned food seemed sensible. Off I went to a nearby 24-hour grocery palace.

As I long ago eschewed home cookery in favour of restaurants, it had been some time since I had visited a supermarket for any reason other than to beg boxes for moving. Imagine my surprise at surveying the vast array of canned possibilities! But however to choose? So I asked myself the question I always pose when I find myself befuddled by the unfamiliar: What would Princess Di do in these circumstances?

Fifteen minutes later, I staggered to the cashier, my Breezway basket overbrimming with tins of smoked oysters and mussels, tins of lobster and crab, tinned patés of French origin, as well as English crackers, dainty relishes, invigorating mustards, and several bottles whose price tags belied the fact that they contained water. Thinking the dog might require some psychic bolstering in the untoward morning that was nearly upon us, I even invested in a large jar of pickled beets.

At home, I settled myself under the comforting arch of a sheltering door frame, surrounded by purchases. The dog rested her head on my lap, and whined.

"Poor thing," I said, prying open the pickled beets and offering her one. She accepted with alacrity.

I woke, sore all over, just after 8:00 a.m. My face was marked with the outline of the tin of smoked oysters I'd used as a pillow. The dog had polished off the pickled beets (500 grams) that I'd neglected to reseal. The earth failed to move. The same could not be said of my four-legged companion.

I called my friend, who had spent the night quite comfortably in his bed. His only explanation was that he had muttered a few words to Albert of Trapani, the saint who is invoked against earthquakes. St. Albert, he added, is also in charge of stiff necks.

"I'll be having a word with him," I said, rubbing my achy joints.

The dog's requirements meant I had to stay close to home. When I thought to console myself with a smoked oyster, I found I didn't have a can opener anyway. So, I ordered in and spent the afternoon looking down from my window to the boulevard, thick with passersby, all of them happy, each and every one blissfully ignorant of their near brush with world-class catastrophe. I envisioned how it all might have been. I sent my dumb imaginings into the world, sowed them among the many other invisibilities that hum without us knowing, everywhere in the air.

secrets of the heart

Whatever else you might say about him, you could never deny that my boyfriend is super organized, especially when it comes to taking vacations. You should see him gear up for a holiday. It's positively Zenlike! Two weeks before departure he begins to scrutinize his wardrobe. He scans his closet, his bureau, with a critical, impartial eye. He grows very still. He touches nothing. He studies each shirt, each pair of trousers. He assigns every garment a rank based on a practicality/desirability ratio. This he determines through a formula he might have invented himself or might have learned from his mother. Who's to say? There are some things you never figure out about a person, no matter how long you're together. An item's versatility, its resistance to wrinkling, its appropriateness to the season, its weight and colour: all these factors are taken into account, are weighed one against another. Hard but necessary choices are made. Before anything is removed from a hanger he folds each garment in his mind, knows just where and how it will fit into his carry-on bag, knows on what day and to just what play or restaurant he will wear such and such a combination. Three days before leaving, he packs. He organizes separate envelopes for such things as tickets, itineraries, hotel brochures. He marks the relevant pages of the guidebooks with coloured Post-it notes. Then he watches with thinly veiled disgust as I rampage around the house fifteen minutes before the airport cab arrives, looking for my passport in the freezer, rooting through laundry hampers trying to find just one more pair of passably salubrious drawers. I don't begrudge him his contempt. He's earned his righteousness. It's true that he thinks of everything. You'd be amazed, the things he thinks of.

"How do you like my shoulders?" he asked. This was a day or two before we set out on a recent jaunt, destination New York.

"They're very nice. They're—they're—quite tanned." I was treading carefully. Obviously, he'd done something to his upper arms to make them noteworthy. But what? Had he sported a tattoo all this time and only just had it removed? How could I have missed such a thing?

"I shaved them. See? They're silky smooth."

I was flabbergasted. In the first place, I've never known him to shave his shoulders, never even thought of them as outstandingly hairy. Furthermore, I don't think I've heard any living soul use the phrase "silky smooth" in a real conversation. It was a little like having something described as "squeaky clean." For a moment, I didn't know where to look.

"I shaved them because I'm planning on wearing that tank top when we're away, and I just can't imagine going around with hairy shoulders."

"Oh. Well. That's nice. I can see. They're certainly smooth. Silky, even."

I didn't let on how bothered I was. What good reason would I have to object? His shoulders are his shoulders. I lay no claim to them. They're his to shave or braid as he sees fit. Even so, I couldn't help but think that he'd worn that damn tank top all summer long, the wiry strands growing up and trailing over his collarbone, all dangly and registering the passing of every breeze, and had he ever so much as once inquired if his hirsute shoulders offended my gaze? No. So, who was he trying to impress with this cosmetic adjustment? Here was a troubling window newly opened on his imaginative life. I could see so plainly how he pictured himself strutting through the East Village; see how he pictured attractive men, more observant than I, lounging in cafés and bars, taking in the passing scene, hunks of burning love who would look him up and down, who would be amazed at his blameless, marmoreal skin. The blood would rush to their loins, the word "alabaster" to their lips. His shoulders would be the talk of New York. I didn't have to listen hard to hear the breaking of commandments.

I might have said something snide had I not just spent the better part of an hour looking wistfully in the mirror, lamenting my naked torso: the whitest torso in all of Christendom, and lardish to boot. While studying my reflection I'd wondered, Is there something I can do to acquire a chest before we go to New York? Is there some way to convince these waist-clinging pendulums to migrate north, to regroup and solidify around my breastbone so that I might have that buffed and sculpted look I've so long craved? Is there some kind of quick fix? An easy implant, a product with a name like "Inflato Pecs"? And whose attention and approbation did I care to garner by being thus configured? My boyfriend's? Or that of the passel of Provincetown poolside pulchritude? Oh, duplicity! Duplicity!

"I've noticed," said my boyfriend, as he folded the tank top and placed it carefully in his bag, "that you don't have any hair around your ankles."

"Socks, I guess. The hair wears away."

"Maybe. But it can also be a sign of heart disease."

"Get out."

"Really. A doctor told me. Something to do with poor circulation."

This was both far-fetched and off-putting. I dismissed it with a long "Hmmmmmm." I didn't say what I wanted to, which is a failing of mine. What I wanted to say was, "Whoa there, chum. How can you tell me what's in my heart if you can't tell me what's in yours?" But maybe that's what we're both learning to do. Anyway, who knows what treacherous path might have been ploughed by such a rejoinder? As peacekeeping initiatives go, I find that avoidance works pretty darn well. So I let it slide. I steered the conversation toward health insurance and ordering tickets for *Rent*. He selected a clean blade. I packed a bulky bathing suit. And the next day, the two of us hit the road.

secrets of the liver

for the longest while I told myself it was a freckle, a surfacing blush of random pigment. Then there came the season, during the heat of the summer, when I was invaded by a spirit of febrile fatalism and roosted on the fantasy that it might be a pretty wee melanoma. Now the sun has passed into Libra, my skin has reclaimed its lardish pallor, and the stains of rain fall plainly on the main. They have washed away such glamorous and innocent prospects, and I am left with only the unsettling and pedestrian truth: it's a liver spot, plain and simple. One of midlife's tattoos. A flat and tawdry emblem of fled youth, of all that has vanished and is irretrievable. A symptom and symbol of my aging. If my right paw were a map of Canada, with the break of the wrist being the 49th parallel, and the base of the knuckles the border with the Territories, this blemish would be Saskatoon. There it sits for all to see, shamelessly straddling the blue vein that is the Saskatchewan River. It is a solitary harbinger of what's in the dermatological offing; for while it is the first such settlement, the lessons of colonial infiltration are plentiful and easy to learn. Other invaders will come along to join it, and this will happen sooner rather than later.

I'm sufficiently vain to be disappointed at this mild eruption, sufficiently realistic not to be surprised. A man in middle age, depending on the slant of light or on the oblique optic angle from which he beholds his reflection, will sometimes have the equilibrium-jarring experience of seeing, all at once and simultaneously, both his boyhood face and the face he will own as an old man shining back at him from the mirror. Latterly, I have observed more and more of what will be my geriatric mask emerging from my here-and-now visage. I was astonished at first to be engaged in some quotidian act of grooming—plucking the weirdly wiry hairs from my eyebrows, say—only to find myself face to face with Grandpa: his hawkish nose, the set of his eyes, his same thin lips, the thrust of his jaw. If I continue to live for as many more years as I have already endured on the earth—two score and change—I will be approaching the age he managed to achieve before caving in. Where I will be and what I will be by that time are, of course, bland mysteries. But as for physiognomy, the writing is well on the wall. I will look just like him, and for this reason, the liver spot—soon to be spots— comes as no surprise. My grandfather's hands, I remember, were mottled with just such a dull plaid, just such blottings from the jottings of Time's hurried Parker.

I refer here to my paternal grandfather. My mother's father died when she was still a teen-ager. I never knew him at all, don't carry a clear image of him in my memory, and have only ever seen one picture of him, as far as I can recall. It was a snapshot of the two of them—my mother, her father—taken by a sidewalk photographer in downtown Calgary sometime in the late thirties or early forties. Strangers though we were, I felt a particular kinship with him when I was growing up. My mother used to tell me how similar we were, temperamentally, and she would not always say this fondly. He was Irish and loquacious and I loved nothing so much as the sound of my own voice, which goes a long way to proving something about the child as father of the man. When I would gas on and on about nothing in particular, my mother would invoke his memory and beg me to shut up. He had other qualities, however, that were worthier of emulation. He was, or so I was told, musical, intelligent, an adventurer, and these were characteristics to which I—who was so like him—was happy to lay claim through simple dint of genetics, even though there was no corroborating evidence of accomplishment or achievement on my part that would substantiate so nervy an appropriation.

For the first 22 years of her life, my mother bore his name. She gave it up—that is, her maiden name—when she married my father and forsook maidenhood and changed her tribal affiliation. She has been a Richardson for close to 50 years now, but I sometimes wonder if, in those vulnerable moments between waking and sleeping, she doesn't sometimes smooth over an existential wrinkle by reminding herself of her origins, by rolling those two syllables—of a name that is really more English than Irish—around on her tongue. Is it part of her secret self? I wonder this in part because, for me, my mother's father's name has taken on an incantatory, occult quality. It is the name I offer up to banks or credit unions when they want some code word they can keep on file and that I can whisper through the glass at a teller to prove to her or him that I am who I say I am. It's the name I use to access such private and magical services as my Internet account. And it was while trying to log on to e-mail, just the other day, that I forgot, for the first time in my thinking life, my mother's maiden name. It wasn't absent long from my memory. It didn't take more than 15 or 20 seconds to retrieve it from those cluttered files. It came back readily enough. I was tired. I was distracted. There might be any number of reasons for such a lapse. Nonetheless, it happened. For a blink or two, that unique identifier, that link to all that history, to all that family, was gone. There was no mirror handy, but had there been, I know very well whose face would have looked out from it. I suspect I could have looked beyond it and seen all the forgetting that's waiting in the wings. As it was, I shook my head and rattled my brain. It surfaced. A surge of relief accompanied that welling. Then all was as it has always been, and I did what I always do. I wrote my grandfather's name using my grandfather's hands.

tweating twoublesome winkles

I am the recent winner—in some insidious raffle draw for which I never bought a ticket—of a mild but lingering virus. Its gift is to sap its host of anything remotely resembling acuity and to visit upon him instead episodes of short-term delirium. So effective has it been at its subversive work that I have had to acknowledge, at least for the time being, that I can no longer rely on my perceptions to provide the foundation for a realistic worldview. Drifting as I do in and out of entertaining, sometimes psychedelic, netherworlds, I am never sure if what I read or hear or see is authentic, or some warped rendering of the truth, the plain facts milled and sluiced through the dull blades of low-grade fever.

The point I want to make is that I may or may not recently have borne witness to the television spot I am about to describe. I cannot, given my addled state, swear to the veracity of what is to follow. I believe I must have been watching *20/20*, for I can distinctly recall Barbara Walters saying, by way of a setup, "And now, we bwing you a fascinating wepowt on a new way of tweating twoublesome winkles!" I may well have hawwucinated—sowwy, I mean hallucinated—the bizarre reportage that followed. It had to do with how plastic surgeons in New York City can't keep up with the demands of clients who are lining up at their doors, begging to regain the complexions of their youth by having botulism injected into their facial furrows. Yup. Botulism. I seem to recall seeing footage that showed the obliging physicians injecting the germ-bearing formula directly into the cosmetically disadvantaged site; into the crow's-feet, say, or into that deep vertical crevice that bifurcates the territory between the eyes and that so many of us of a certain age carry about.

It was, I think, a Canadian ophthalmologist—don't ask why or how—who discovered the smoothing utility of so unlikely an intervention. The botulism effectively knees the wrinkle—or the muscle that causes it—in the groin and keeps it paralysed for a few months. As the only apparent function of these muscles is to bunch up and make wrinkles possible, you can safely take them out of

commission without any possibility of harming the overall mecha-
nism. When the poison eventually releases its hold, as eventually it
must, and the wrinkle starts to reappear, the patient need only
return for a botulistic booster shot or top-up. Key to the success of
this therapy, of course, is the amount of the damaging agent intro-
duced into the system. It must be minuscule enough that its effect is
highly localized. Otherwise, it might be lured away from the
crow's-feet to which it is assigned and into the gut, where its effect
would be more deleterious than beneficial.

"Medicine! Don't it just beat all," I thought. At least, I think
that's what I think I thought once the show was done and I made
my way to the bathroom for another round of joyful purging.
When the water was flushed clear again, I remained on my knees,
the better to study my face reflected back from that still and porce-
lain pool. I couldn't help but notice how the grievous crease
between my eyes was growing ever deeper. Nothing a little injec-
tion of botulism can't freshen up, I thought, donning my bathrobe
and fuzzy slippers and nipping down the street to the nearby park,
where there are many jettisoned syringes available for the taking. I
selected one that seemed in pretty good shape, took it home,
bleached and boiled it—you can't be too careful these days—and
then had a reconnoitre of the fridge. Lo and behold, there was a
significant quantity of potato salad left over from the summer and
stored in an improperly sealed container, as well as several vats of
spinach dip that had seen better days sometime last year and some
stuffing from last Christmas's turkey. Each of these seemed to me
to be potentially crawling with all manner of toxic agents, some of
which might be botulistic. I dumped the whole pungent mess into
the blender, gave it a long whirl, extracted a needleful of promis-
ing-looking liquid, and injected it right into the offending fold. I
gave a few squirts to my crow's-feet, too.

At least, I think this is what I did. I believe I also applied some of
the goo as a facial mask. At least, I believe that is what I found
thickly encrusted all over my puss when I awoke 24 hours later.
There is so very much of which I can't be 100 per cent certain,
given my present condition and all. However, my eyebrows have
entered a state of paralysis and when I sweat I smell like mayon-
naise and the last time I looked I had the complexion of a man half
my age. Or do I mean twice my age? Numbers. They're always the

first to go. Apropos, I thought I should call *20/20* to let them know about my dilemma, if that is what it is, but my computer doesn't have "Walters" in its spell checker, which throws everything into doubt, and will they know to whom I refer if I call up and ask for "Barbara Wallets"? Which I now believe to be her real name. Anyway, someone should know about the gnawing at my love handles, which I believe to be the flesh-eating disease I think I may have injected into my navel in a moment of devil-may-care bravado. Help me, Bawbwa. I'm shwinking! Not that she'd give a good goddamn. Not that she'd take the trouble to turn her perfect face and cast a pitying glance at sods like me, sinking deep in her tewwible twail of destwuction.

doomed proposals: 2

Creaky joints in the morning. Hair and gums in a breakneck race for recession. Long and deepening trenches furrowing the face. Don't think for a minute these symptoms of aging trouble me. Happily, happily do I cleave to the antique maxim recorded in that profound tract, *Desiderata*; gladly, gladly do I surrender the things of youth. The only winnowing that brings on pangs is the dimming of intelligence. Commonplace facts and skills that were part of my daily arsenal have eroded beyond recuperation. Long division? Gone for good. The life cycle of the fruit fly? Don't even ask. When was the War of 1812? How the hell should I know?

I felt this crumbling most keenly the other day when I was in Value Village, shopping for formal wear, and happened upon an old cub scout uniform. The shirt sleeves were festooned with badges: cunningly designed crests attesting to the multitude of talents possessed by the gifted lad who once wore it. I could have wept. I too was a cub scout. I too once sported, for all the world to see, the outward evidence of my competence in housekeeping, birdwatching, carpentry, path finding, first aid, musicianship, Morse code, and semaphore. Once, I could identify deer scat at 20 paces. Once, I knew which side of the tree was favoured by moss. Gone.

All gone. I went home and spent the rest of the day in bed with a cold compress on my brow.

I was bemoaning this to a patient friend who circulates on the sunny side of life's wide boulevard. She made the point that, while we can no longer be reliably counted on to start a fire by rubbing a couple of sticks together, there are nonetheless compensatory adult capabilities that accrue over time.

"Why," she said brightly, "now you can distinguish a cappuccino from a latte! That's something, *n'est-ce pas?* Of course, no one is going to give you a badge for it. Which is a pity."

She's right, of course. And so I come before you today, my friends, to advance this modest proposal. Someone, somewhere, at some level of administration, should implement a program that will award badges to grownups. These would be symbols of growth and learning, tokens we could wear on our sleeves, signals to the world that we are steeped in accomplishment.

Why, there's a bottomless well of potential categories! Who wouldn't be proud to decorate a blazer with the Pasta Identification Badge, a triangular swatch appliquéd with a plate of oddly configured noodles. It would be awarded for being able to distinguish capellini from fettucini from ziti from spaghetti. A special commendation would be issued to those who could confidently pronounce, as well as identify, "gnocchi."

Imagine a crest emblazoned with a five-dollar bill. This is the Tipping Badge, presented to those who confidently and comfortably, without blushing or looking away or muttering inanities, bestow gratuities on spa attendants, hairdressers, pedicurists, and other service personnel. The badge will be edged in gold if the applicant can prove that she has not held up a party of 12, while figuring out, with a pocket calculator, 15 per cent on each individual's lunch bill.

I envision a badge decorated with an elephant perched upon an egg. This is the Grace under Pressure award, given to those who comport themselves calmly in life's awkward circumstances. For instance, you get into an elevator and detect a bad smell. At the next floor, half a dozen people get on and wrinkle their noses. If you blush and say, "It wasn't me!" you don't qualify for this one.

Oh, my friends! Now my heart has taken wing! Many are the possibilities for grownup badges! The Pilot Light Reignition Badge,

the Mutual Fund Comprehension Badge, the Compliment Accep-
tance Badge, the Self-Actualization Badge, the Intelligent Use of
Credit Badge, the Polite but Firm with Phone Solicitors Badge, the
Never Walks along Robson Street while Talking on a Cellular
Phone Badge, and a nice little badge for anyone who read *Middle-
march* or *The Age of Innocence* before they came to the screen.

All of society will benefit from this plan! Employment will be
created for designers and examiners. The desperate will have a new
lease on life. We'll all have a fresh reason to get out of bed in the morning. Don't fight it. It's an idea whose time has come. It comes straight
from my heart which, for the nonce, is all I am wearing on my sleeve.

sleep habits of the stars

Middle age brings the dawning
of wisdom. You come to understand that there is a reason for
everything. You understand that love handles have a kind of aero-
dynamic utility in that they slow us when we're jogging, thus
relieving the stress the brain must endure when it jounces around
in its pan; that the furrows around the eyes are a useful place to
plant a spare crop of canola; that receding gums were meant to
hasten the progress of dentistry, which in turn has residual effects
on the space program. But far and away the most alluring aspect of
reaching forty-in-the-shade is that every so often the morning mail
contains a clear signal that one has arrived. Perhaps it comes in the
form of a banker's letter, full of sly insinuations vis-à-vis the Visa
gold card and the heady joys available to those who are eligible to
carry such a passport to bliss. Or maybe the ticket to the promised
land of vaunted social status comes as a billet-doux from the editor
of the *Economist*, a highly personalized epistle which says boldly
that you, William Richardson, have been exclusively selected, from
a very broad swath of the population, as one who might benefit
from a yearly subscription to this highly influential publication.
Does the editor know that William Richardson's bank balance
hovers perpetually in the mid-three-figure range? Does the editor
know that William Richardson's stomach shrivels into something

the size and texture of a walnut when he hears the words "supply side"? What does it matter? For William has arrived!

All of this pales in comparison to the recent frisson of accomplishment enjoyed by William Richardson when the letter carrier dropped off Ikea's "Sleep Habits of the Stars" survey. Does it not make your DNA uncoil with wonder? Ikea! That crafty purveyor of Swedish furniture, thanks to whose good offices every buyer of knockdown furniture has a kitchen drawer overbrimming with allen wrenches! Yes! That very same Ikea has identified William Richardson as a Star, and wants to know how he sleeps!

Jennifer Sexton, who was thoughtful enough to send William Richardson the survey, says the responses she garners from "musicians, politicians, business professionals, members of the media, sports heros [sic], movie stars and some of our best read authors" will be compiled and correlated with the confessions of assorted U.S. superstars, and that the results will then be used as part of an Ikea promotion for their bedroom furniture. Furthermore, those who provide "particularly scintillating" answers to the 21 questions just might have their very own names used in the ad! Zowee!

The queries reflect that freewheeling tell-all attitude the Swedes embrace when it comes to bedroom matters. They include such probes as "Do you watch TV before going to bed?" and "What is the strangest place you've ever slept?" and "When you sleep with someone do you most often keep your distance or are you a cuddler?" as well as the Barbara Walters–esque "If your bed could talk, what would it say?" There are also multiple-choice options. For instance, Ikea would like to know if, in order to fall asleep, William prefers hot milk or hot sex. They are also curious to learn whether William would rather sleep with a pet or with the man/woman he met that night.

In fact, William Richardson would be more inclined to sleep with the pet he met that night, does not have a chatty box spring, has a dairy intolerance, and has found that a good way to avoid getting overheated during sex is to remove his clothes. But he is willing to overlook these minor quibbles and assist Ikea in its study if they are able to provide him with just a wee bit of clarification. That is, have they contacted him in his capacity as a politician, a musician, a movie star, or a sports hero? This is important information, because it could well change the complexion of his answers. To wit:

As a politician (elected vice-president of his eighth-grade class), William Richardson's snoozing choices are dictated by the techniques he learned as a student at the Jean and Aline Chrétien School of Self-Defence. He sleeps with an Inuit sculpture handy to the bed in order to clout trespassers before administering the well-loved face grab. As a musician (received fourth place in the Kiwanis Music Festival, 1964, for his piano performance of "Little Birch Canoe"), William Richardson chooses to sleep on sheets that are appliquéd with the score of the Brahms "Lullaby." William often sings himself to sleep, which also answers the "Do you sleep alone or with someone?" inquiry. As a movie star, William Richardson's career is mostly distinguished by the fact that he once stood next to Glenn Close at a Granville Island cheese shop. He turned to her and said, "Feta Attraction?" She pretended not to hear. Often, William puts himself to sleep at night by replaying the scene over and over in his head. As a sports hero, William sometimes dreams of how he stopped his own bleeding when he cut himself on his skates a few years back. He has been known to dispel early-morning depression by simply recalling the triumphant day he bench-pressed almost 60 pounds.

Furthermore, William would like to say that he long ago determined that in the highly unlikely event that something should transpire in the bedroom that would lead to his achieving paternity, he would do whatever he could to see that the child was named after an Ikea product. Isn't there a bookcase they call Billy?

William Richardson thanks Ikea for thinking of him, and looks forward to receiving the clarification he requires in order to complete the "Sleep Habits of the Stars" survey. His deepest wish is that when the results are tabulated and mixed up with the responses of American superstars, he will somehow find himself sleeping next to Richard Gere, who might actually enjoy the Brahms "Lullaby."

doomed proposals: 3

Men! Are you alarmed when you read of fertility studies (*cf. The New Yorker*, January 15, 1996) conducted all over the world (by Skakkebaek in Denmark, by Nelson and Bunge in Iowa, by Jouannet in Paris) which demonstrate that sperm counts are undergoing a global plummeting? Does it make you feel testy (no pun intended!) to know that the same studies show that the sperm you *do* produce might well be in some vital way defective: deformed, twisted, and slow? Do you furrow your brow at the news that no one has been able to pinpoint the reason for this fallow season? Are you fretful that you might be one of the millions of fellows whose breeding prospects are diminished because of so perplexing and invidious a dwindling? Are you sacrificing sleep to the terrible fear that you might therefore never preserve the family line, might never create another being in your own image unto whom you can disburse your splendid nose and your particular talent for backgammon? Hmmmmm? Well, then! Would you be interested to hear that all is not as bleak as it might seem at first glance? Would you be heartened to learn of a startling new product that will enable you to make the very best use of the few decent sperm left to you after the deleterious effects of stress and pollutants have weighed in? Then read on! Your lucky day is at hand!

Ah Come Now Enterprises (Acne) is pleased to announce the joyful release (so to speak) of SPASM: Sperm Plan for the Averagely Sexed Man. Acne's SPASM is a kit that contains everything you'll require to train your sperm to work for you! No longer need you be held ransom by the frenzied whims of those wee and wiggling worms! No! Fairly controlled experiments conducted by generally qualified scientists in relatively clean laboratories have proven more or less conclusively that by simply learning a few easy-to-master techniques and commands, you can coach your own seed, regardless of how scanty and withered it might be, to storm the walls of even the most standoffish ovum! This is not a correspondence course! You will never need to attend a class or speak to an instructor! It's easier than macramé, and a heckuva lot more fun, too! All you need to get you going is the Acne SPASM starter set and the magazine or video of your choice! Still interested? Then read some more!

Acne's SPASM will allow you to:

Do your own sperm count in the privacy of your own room by using the patented WANK (Worried about No Kids?) technique. Once you've learned WANK, you're halfway home! Your kit comes fully equipped with a microscope and slides that will allow you to do a tally of your sperm. You'll study the cunning ways and habits of sperm, learn that every sperm is as individuated and distinct from its fellows as are seamen (no pun intended!) on a ship! Why, you'll want to give them names to match their personalities. Sleepy, Dozy, Grumpy, Dasher, Dancer, Blitzen, and so on!

Once you've come to know your sperm, and to feel at one with those happy uterine voyagers, you'll be ready to move on to the most challenging and rewarding part of SPASM's program: the patented JERK (Jumping Estrogen! Ready, Kids?) technique for actually training your sperm! Yes! Recent research is on the verge of demonstrating fairly conclusively that sperm is actually every bit as responsive to training commands as is the family pooch! More so, even! If you can teach Fido to sit and play dead, then you can teach your sperm to stand up and look alive! Really! It's a little-known fact that each and every spermatozoon has an IQ that would put a dolphin to shame. Sperm is highly voice-responsive and obedience-friendly. Why, all you really need to do to achieve the desired results is train yourself! With a little discipline and forethought, it's easy to manage! You need simply be prepared for that happy moment when the long-tailed replicating agents exit the station (not to be coy!) and go rushing to catch that all-important streetcar named ovum. Then, when they are still within earshot, you need only shout out blasts of encouragement such as: "Go for it, guys! Storm the Bastille! Remember the Alamo!" Be assured that even if there aren't quite as many sperm rushing for the eager egg as would have been the case a generation ago, those that are on the case are trying twice as hard. It takes a bit of practice to wean yourself away from such tried-and-true expostulations as "Oh, Jesus!" or "Help me, Rhonda!" But you won't be sorry you did!

So much of fertility is psychological, and Acne's SPASM kit comes with enclosures that will give you that vital mental edge. None of these tokens is gratuitous. Rather, they are based on all the latest scientific surveys. For instance, the Finns have one of the highest sperm counts in the world, and studies undertaken in Finland show that men who are better educated and have more money have higher sperm counts still! Therefore, the kit includes a framed replica of a University of Helsinki Master's degree to hang on the wall by your love nest! Furthermore, it's been learned that long-term prisoners, for some indecipherable reason, have extraordinarily high sperm counts. Taking advantage of this intelligence, the kit includes a T-shirt that reads "My grandparents visited Sing Sing and all they brought me back was this stupid T-shirt." Slap that on your chest, and the old count will go up exponentially. You can count on it!

There's much more to Acne's SPASM kit. It's easy! It's fun! And it ensures the continuance of the human species, too! Buy one tonight at a registered pharmacy. And while you're at it, pick up a few boxes of Pampers. You'll need 'em, fella!

aids: four paragraphs

1. The Germans—who can say why—have a real gift for coining *Schadenfreude* kinds of expressions which classify emotional states that are both hybrid and less than honourable. Pity mixing it up with joy. Envy alloying itself with glee. Nostalgia bleeding into loathing. And so on. I wonder if they've cobbled together the syllables that describe the unsettling mix of grief and envy that washes over me when talk turns, as it so often has over the last dozen years, to AIDS. It oozes up when someone invokes what I think of as the most intimate symbol of the scourge: the address book that was once a catalogue of friendship and has now become a death register. Once, there were three hundred names. One by one, they have been deleted. The pages are a mess of erasures and striations. I imagine those small, smudged leaves, imagine the enormity, the flesh-crushing weight of each individual's suffering, imagine the burgeoning sorrow and loneliness of the one left behind. I imagine this and think, how terrible. And I imagine this and think, how lucky. How lucky to have had so many comrades, how lucky to have been so involved, how lucky to have been so often privy to the terrible vibrancy of dying. How lucky to have been so needed. Shame intrudes on this noxious cocktail of sensibilities. Selfishly, I hold up my own whitewashed days for comparison. For I don't even keep an address book. For I gird myself against the world, insulate myself from its crueller currents with brittleness and occupation. For I hold back, stand outside the circle, haven't known or seen or held the dying. And shouldn't I therefore number myself among the blessed? And what is this envy that comes slipping through the cracks of grief? And how can I own or name something as execrable as this?

2. I used to be an habitué of a men's sauna called the Garden Baths. This was years back. This was when I was young, unpartnered, when I was horny all the time. Conveniently, I lived only a block or two away. I'd just pop on over of an evening, often with my downstairs neighbour, Bob. In we'd go and doff our clothes and don our towels and trundle off on our separate prowls, padding up and down the dim hallways, squinting into the narrow, subfusc chambrettes, checking out the steamroom, hoping to enter into some pleasant, short-term contract. For Bob, it usually worked out. Bob had a talent for the baths. He understood the lingo, the etiquette, the slow, decorous dance. It helped that he was cute. I was hopeless. I never knew what to say or where or how to stand. What was more, I wore very unbecoming glasses. You can take it from me that Dorothy Parker's aphorism about corrective lenses and men who make passes is all too true. So, mostly I'd just retire to my room and arrange myself in a provocative pose on the little cot the management provided for assignations. I felt like a seal waiting to get harpooned. I'd amuse myself by thinking of how the French for seal is *"phoque."* Only rarely did some rube walk into my parlour. Mostly, I'd just lie there and listen to the sounds of lovemaking coming through the pressboard walls of the grim little cubicle. Bob would call the next day and tell me about his many triumphs. I begrudged him nothing. This was 1978, the year before he went back to Australia. For a while we kept in touch. I thought I should try to find him in 1993 when the baths burned to the ground. I knew he'd be amused by the biblical richness of such a conflagration. But I didn't even try to track him down. I just didn't want to know.

3. Okay. We all know you can get AIDS from carelessly sharing needles or from the drip of tainted blood or from some such accident or oversight or misfortune. But most people I've known who have been afflicted almost certainly got it from fucking. Similarly, most of the people I know who have babies got them from fucking. Poor old fucking! What a terrible burden it carries. We impute to it

everything that's evil and degenerative as well as everything that's rich and procreative. Is this fair? Sometimes I'm overtaken by a glimmer of insight, by a small, still voice that says, "Wait a second. What's this good and bad stuff? If ever there was anything in and of itself that's wholly impartial, it would be fucking. Fucking is fucking, plain and simple. Everything else is something we've made up." Sometimes, I think I'm on the cusp of understanding something. But that's as far as I can push it. I'm just not smart enough to push it through to meaning. And anyway, I'd rather be shopping.

4. I love to hear a chanteuse in a live recording, love to hear Edith Piaf or Judy Garland or Barbra Streisand work the crowd, whip them up into an emotional froth. I love to be manipulated in so overt, harmless a way. There's one such disk I especially enjoy, a recording of Barbara Cook at Carnegie Hall that was made round about 1983. Barbara Cook is one of those singers gay guys of a certain generation love: a hefty soprano with a crystalline voice, a real gift for cabaret and show tunes. She's a cult object, really, and her adherents just can't get enough. That night, at Carnegie, she held the audience in the palm of her elegant, chubby hand. She milked them of feeling, basked in the roar of their approval, all these male voices lusty and cheering. That was 16 years ago, in New York City. Sometimes, when I listen to the concert, I wonder what the room would look like if there could be a little light shining above the head of every man there who would be dead before the decade was out. Sometimes, I wonder how raucous the applause would be if there were a reunion of that same audience. What is the sound of one hand clapping? Sometimes, I entertain such macabre imaginings. Mostly, I enjoy the music, both the joyful and the sad. Mostly, I live in the minute. Mostly, I believe it will go on.

beloved

Beloved friend:
Some people, when they're not long for the world, long for the world. I'm thinking of your friend who died today and who

wouldn't go gently. Feistiness at the close of day is commendable, even stirring. But this man's campaign against inevitability was distinguished by garish vigour. His blunt stubbornness, the opiates, and the virus that had scaled his brain stem nullified the testimony of his own body. None of the plain evidence was admissible. He was unmoved by the frankness of physicians and by the persuasive indignities visited on him. Not incontinence, not fever, not the weird and shifting lesions that grew on his skin like unchartable islands, not the masks his visitors wore, not the attachments and contrivances, the pumps and the tubes; not even his grotesquely swollen legs or mottled lungs would make him admit that immortality was, at best, a remote possibility.

Denial was a great preservative. You were there when he whispered to his mother that he blamed it all on that blood transfusion. You listened to his ever more revisionist tellings of his own history, his tidying up of the past. You heard him instruct his doctors to pull out every stop and leave in every plug. They were to do whatever they could to ensure his continuance.

"He's taking his time," you'd say, worn out with worry and with guilty impatience. For weeks on end you had been visiting: once, sometimes twice a day. Willingly, you juggled schedules, fought traffic, jockeyed for parking, talked with him, listened to him, went at his bidding on quixotic runs for Thai food, for sushi. The doctors used words like "virulent" and "invasive" and "galloping" and "palliative." He phoned and made a plane reservation home for Christmas. He renewed his subscriptions. "He's taking his time," you'd say, admiring and alarmed.

But he didn't so much take time as eviscerate it. He beat it thin. He stretched it out. He didn't care a fig for convenience or seemliness. It is fashionable now for the dying to summon their nearest and dearest to their bedsides, to look about the room in a resigned way and signal for the hemlock. He didn't give a damn for fashion. Nor did he give a damn for the expectations we foist on the dying: that we will learn something from them, that they will give us comfort. He didn't give a damn about transfiguration, or the dawning of wisdom, or tunnels made of light, or the quiet joy of surrender. It is possible that, after a time, he didn't give a damn about you, or about any of the court who danced attendance, except to demand that you all be there, that you play your supporting role in the seemingly unending drama of his hanging on.

I never knew this man. I am divining all this from what you told me, and from reading between the lines of your discreet reports. You met him when he was healthy. Nothing in your friendly and collegial relationship would have suggested the evolution of so grim a bonding. Nothing would suggest that he would become, in the end, a burden.

What does she get from this? I would ask myself, when you would drop by on your way to or from the hospital with grim news to report. Today, 12 hours after his dying, after you'd been up all night making phone calls, making arrangements, you said, "I wonder how much of this was a kind of penance for not being there when my father died?"

I could have offered the usual comforts and blandishments: that your father was ninety-something; that he had, relatively speaking, an easy death; that he was, after all, in Australia. I didn't, because it seemed a colossal vanity to suggest that I might dam up the source of your real and pointless guilt by cooing a few platitudes. But I should have said what I'm saying to you now—that none of your deep-rooted reasons obviate the shining fact that you cared for this prickly man. You were unfailingly there as his friend and advocate because you are, first and foremost and simply, a good person. You are as good a person as ever I've met; and real goodness isn't changed or altered or even illuminated by looking into its pathology.

You said, "He was still in the bed when I got to the hospital. His mouth was still open, like he was trying to gasp after his last breath. I think that's the image that will stay with me."

Here's the image that will stay with me. It's a rainy afternoon, late in October. In a moment of unaccountable lucidity, your friend has decided to plan his funeral. He's asked you to take him chapel shopping. He is on his scooter, and you are trotting along beside him on Burrard Street, holding an umbrella in one hand and pushing his oxygen pole with the other. You are stepping off the curb when the tube connecting the oxygen to his impoverished blood supply slips out. He howls, in anger, panic, and pain. You are standing in the pouring rain, trying to reinsert the tube, trying to hold the umbrella, trying to offer comfort, trying to cross the intersection, trying not to mind that he is cursing you, trying not to laugh, trying not to cry. You are tender and concerned. You can't wait for this to be over. You are looking forward to sitting down, later the same day, and telling someone this story.

canadian gothic

Autumn comes and every year it's the same goddamn thing. I roll around in nostalgia like a dog in a stinking seal carcass. God almighty! If only I could reclaim the hours I waste practising attractive and resolute postures of wistfulness. It's just so pathetic! Why, you should see the way I sit at the table, with my several chins in my hand, studying the changing habits of the dwindling light, all the while enumerating lost friends, fled lovers, mislaid coffee mugs, lapsed magazine subscriptions, and so on. Every so often, a sensible voice oozes up through the Freudian layers, claws its way through the sticky strata of id, super-ego, ego, and intrudes on my reverie. "Yoo-hoo! Bill! Wake up! Reality check! Who do you imagine is directing this scene? Ingmar Bergman, for chrissake? Look around! There ain't no cameras, Bibi Andersson doesn't have your number, Max von Sydow wouldn't take the time to lance you if you were a boil on his butt! So get over it!"

But I shove the kill-joy pedant back down, I pay him no heed, I pour another cup of tea, I kiss my own reflection in the mirror, I whisper «*Bonjour tristesse!*» to my image (made all hazy by the steam rising from the mug), and then recline on the sofa. Recumbent and full of a rootless longing, I listen to French and melancholy music—Satie, Debussy. I fold my arms across my chest and imagine funerals: my parents', my dog's, my own. Mostly my own. Oh! It makes me quite wet-eyed when I see how it all will be. It's so clear to me! A chill church. The thin light of January angled through stained glass. A couple of friends and a few of my more persistent detractors, each sucking on the bitter lozenge of their individual regrets. There they are, along with the curious strangers, a cunning realtor or two hoping to make nice with the estate executor just in case there's something in it for them, and the rubbies who have come in out of the cold hoping for a kind word or a sandwich or an open casket so they might view someone who is worse off than they and possibly snitch a cravat or a pair of pawnable cuff links. I see the wreaths, the arrangements, the perfumed cascades of blooms: none of that "in lieu of flowers" shit for me, not on your life. On my life. Which, I must never, never forget, is already half over. Tears chart a course from duct to lips. I am disappointed when I taste them. They are never salty enough.

This fall, for the first time, I have my little yard: a new and public arena for this soggy, seasonal self-indulgence. How satisfying to survey the big elm that shades the boulevard, to watch while its overhanging branches disabuse themselves of their used-up leaves! How moving, when their assiduous days of photosynthesizing are done, to see them clatter to earth, among the damp gum wrappers and crumpled Safeway flyers! I listen to the Mantovani orchestra play "Les Feuilles Mortes" until there are a dozen or more brown discards on the lawn. Then I trot out with my rake, and when I have swept for a minute or two, I give myself over to the business of leaning. I lean on the rake like a guileless rustic, like something right out of Hardy, and stare into the middle distance. I lean on the rake and heave an autumnal sigh and think about my many lost opportunities and the places I'll never go and the books I'll never read. It makes my nipples go rigid with pleasure. And sometimes, while I am thus engaged, the very embodiment of Canadian Gothic, one of the old fellers, one of the old codgers who lives in the neighbourhood, will come along and size me up as someone who'd like nothing better than a chinwag about the past.

"Well, I moved here back in '37, bought that corner lot and built on it, lived in the same house ever since, except for the war of course, lived there with the wife till she died, it'll be nine years ago next Tuesday now that I think of it, yes, nine years since she passed on, seen lots of changes of course, lots of changes on the street, yes, all those Vancouver specials coming up now, but they're good neighbours, very clean and all, and I've slowed up quite a bit since the wife, you know, so mostly these days I just look after my garden, yes, it's doing very well although the roses all came up with the black spot this year what with the terrible wet spring and all, no, I didn't think I'd have a single bloom, but it all worked out fine, well, I must be going, I see you've got some raking to do."

He walks away on his bowed legs, two inches shorter than when he was my age, his straw boater pulled down around his ears. And I feel a surge of something like optimism, for it won't be long before enough years go by that my whole life will be suffused with autumn, autumn, autumn, though for the moment in what passes for my own garden there's not one single rose, just a discarded apple, oozing, and two wasps tumble on it, addled by fermentation, by the waning year, and the Sweet 100s are numbering their reddening beads, their leaves already tattered, already heady with the promise of rot, everything is starting to unravel, everything is so redolent, this is the catechism of ending, so sweet, so sad, it makes me almost delirious with need, with joy, with the longing that it will go on and on, forever and ever, amen.

speed bumps

They've gone and laid down speed bumps in the alley behind the Buddhist temple. Quite who "they" might be, I can't say. Oh, in a literal sense I'm sure the job was done by workers employed by the city, a cheerful, unionized crew well pleased with their benefits package, fully equipped with all the necessary tools, expertise, permits, and time required to oversee so total and telling a transformation in the complexion of the asphalt. But at whose urging was it done? Whence came the impetus? Did council strike a committee to study the situation city-wide and produce a list of alleys where the installation of such inhibitors to automotive celerity would be beneficial to the common good? Was it a neighbourhood initiative that got the ball rolling, a consortium of concerned citizens who were vexed by the vehicular velocity up and down the laneway? Or were the bumps built at the behest of the Buddhists themselves? I favour the latter hypothesis, for no other reason than that I first remarked the things round about the time I noticed that a gift shop had opened in that self-same holy place.

The idea of such a gift shop disturbed me somehow. I walk on thin ice when I say this, for I know very little about Buddhism. In

fact, I am still unable to spell the word with anything like reliabil-
ity, can never remember where the consonants double up. In this
deficiency I am unique in my circle, for I am just about the only
person I know who hasn't made the switch over to one branch of
Buddhism or another in the last couple of years. Dharma, Vipas-
sana, Kagyu, Nyingma: such arcane utterances as these now lard
conversations with my pals, where once Latte, Americano, and
Cappuccino sufficed. Frankly, I'm not at all sure why so many of
my friends, co-workers, and acquaintances are now calling themselves Buddhists, as it seems to have made no difference whatsoever to anyone's outward appearance or actions. None of them
look any more serene. As near as I can tell, they're still the same
flesh-gnawing, fly-swatting, fuck-this, fuck-that dyspeptics they
were back in the days when, if pressed, they would identify their
affiliation as Anglican or U.C., probably adding the qualifier
"lapsed." Of course, it is possible there are now facets of their lives
they keep hidden from me, since I'm an outsider and all. Perhaps
they have sworn some vow that prevents them from confessing
that the hours they used to devote to downloading questionable
material from the Net they now give over to banging those little
cymbals in rooms thick with incense and memorizing Ginsberg
poems. Maybe their dreams have all gone the colour of saffron. I
have no way of knowing, and anyway it's not the point. I was getting around to saying why the gift shop in the Buddhist temple
made me uneasy, and I think it has to do with what I perceive as an
ideological incompatibility. I'd always understood that a basic
tenet of Buddhism was that desire created pain, and that therefore
one should free oneself from unprincipled longings that get in the
way of bliss. It's a good idea, and easy to defend, but it hardly fits
hand in glove with the concept of "gift shop." I have never been in
an institutional gift shop of any description that was not meant to
sow and nurture desire where none should ever, ever grow. I mean,
is there a person on earth who deeply, deeply needs a kitchen witch
or still more potpourri? Yet how many times, and in how many gift
shops, have we allowed ourselves to be deluded into thinking we,
or someone we know, might be possessed of just such a requirement? Compounding this glaring discrepancy in the present
instance were the speed bumps that appeared contemporaneous
with the opening of said chotchke emporium. Could it be that their

purpose is to enhance the possibility that slow-moving drivers might notice the new boutique and, as long as they're decelerating anyway, consider stopping and checking it out? The more I thought about it, the more I was convinced this was the case. Lord love a duck, how crafty can you get!

I am happy to report that my apprehensions were considerably alleviated by simply visiting the Buddhist gift shop and noting that, at least on the day I dropped in, there was nothing there anyone could possibly want or even imagine wanting. A few small statues. A pendant or two. Some tokens of indeterminate purpose that may have been bookmarks. And that was just about it. Four grim ladies stood with their hands behind their backs and gave discouraging looks to anyone who wandered in. Desire? What desire? Such a clever stratagem! To pull the rug out from under false longings in the very place where they are meant to prosper! A memorable lesson of almost homeopathic potency. And it worked, too. As I say, I know nothing about Buddhism, but even I felt the nudgings of satori as I left without so much as reaching for my wallet.

I decided to take the back way home, just to see if the speed bump trend is spreading. It is not, nor was there any sign of anything like speed in any of the narrow lanes I wandered. But I was in a mood for enlightenment, and I found it everywhere. I noted some graffiti on the back of a store: "I was here and now I'm gone, I've left my boogers to turn you on." I began to chant it, as though it were a venerable koan. I saw a dog achieving union with some uncovered trash. In garden after garden, runner beans were beginning their patient ascent up their assigned poles. The ripening scent of compost mingled with the honeyed waft of roses, and then they were as one. On impulse, I walked up the alley behind our house, entered the garage—where I never go—and had a poke through a box of books set aside for discard. On top was an anthology of sacred poetry. I opened it at random and read this, by the Buddhist poet Ryokan:

> When we see clearly, the great teachings are the same.
> What can ever be lost? What can be attained?

How perfect, under the circumstances. It was a sign. I couldn't believe I had consigned this collection to rummage! Longing welled up in my heart. I was filled again with desire. What else had I got rid of in some intemperate tidy fit? I went through the box and reclaimed fully half of those books. I was my old self again. I'd been away. Now I was home, and happy to be there.

deacquisition

The urge to purge has surged. I can feel it welling, this seasonal longing that always takes me over round about this time of year. I mean the need to divest myself of books. Why books and why now? Something about the gloomy nights of November makes me want to liberate myself from such encumbrances: "volumes of forgotten lore," needless chattels that might subvert a spontaneous whim to chuck it all over and hightail it outta here. For Mexico, say. While so capricious a notion has yet to overtake me, I can imagine easily enough how it might. As prospects for change or improvement diminish, commensurate with each year's passing, I grow ever more alert to how I might be approaching the moment the Possibility of flight makes so a per-suasive case for itself that it will become a Necessity. And so, in order that I'm ready to fold my tents, I rid myself of books.

Such a winnowing was once a rare undertaking, and I found it hellishly difficult. Every book had a history, a reason. I could recall the exact circumstances of its purchase or presentation; could call to mind where I was, with whom I was, when I acquired and/or read the thing. It was a touchstone, an attachment. Inevitably, every 18 months or so, the day would come when I would be brought face to face with the fact that there were considerably more books than there was shelf space to accommodate them, and something of a practical, redressing nature would have to be done. I would spend hours and hours at the sad chore, picking books up and turning them over, holding them in my hands, weighing the virtues of one against the other, balancing usefulness and necessity against fond fancy and the possibility that one day the information contained therein (a natural history of the bat, an encyclopedia of cake decorating) might come in handy. Even when I couldn't make a case for keeping a book because of what it contained, I was happy enough to grant it a stay of banishment just because it was attractive. I was as much in love with the books as objects as I was with the narratives that were at home within them.

As life and career progressed—wound on, anyway—the books started arriving unbidden. Reader's copies, final page proofs, bound galleys: all the items that come your way when you interview writers or review books or otherwise paddle around the fringes of the publishing world. At first, I was delighted to be the recipient of such largesse. Over time, I found myself reading more and more out of professional obligation than out of any debt owed to pleasure. Not surprisingly, a dumb, self-protective forgetfulness began to settle in. I would look at the books queued up in their ranks and see how the lines of their spines were fading, one into the other.

Volume breeds familiarity, and we all know what familiarity breeds. Once, I held texts as sacred objects and could not bring myself to part with them. Now, I cull with indifference. If I cast a Lot's wife look over my shoulder, I can see at a glance a dozen books that are ripe for harvesting. I won't hesitate, and I know that a few months hence I won't regret the absence of old biographies of Montgomery Clift and Anthony Trollope, a history of the hurdy-gurdy, and the *Little, Brown Book of Anecdotes*. There are many more just like them, and soon enough they too will be disappeared.

Lest you think me irredeemably callous, chill, and cavalier in this regard, I will offer in my defence the news that I am still capable of small shows of sentimentality. For instance, I draw the line at dumping personalized copies. If some writer has inscribed his or her work to me, I will always find room for it on my groaning Ikea shelves, however irrelevant the book might be to my interests or needs. I do this for no other reason than to forestall the day that that same writer is rooting through a secondhand store and discovers my treachery. I had such an experience myself, quite recently, and I can tell you, it's on a par with finding your book twice marked down in the bottom of a remainder bin.

As well, there are a few books from my childhood to which I cling: Kipling's *Just So Stories* and one of the "Happy Hollisters" series, for example. These I also guard because of their flyleaf inscriptions. It is my own name I find written there, set down by me in a long-ago, proprietary moment; my own name, its letters neatly formed and connected; my own name, spelled out in my clear, careful, guileless schoolboy script of more than 30 years ago. Recently, for no good reason, when I had come across those old books, I tried to forge my 10-year-old signature. The body has a long memory, and I was not long in achieving a reasonable facsimile of those solid, dull strokes. The physical task of writing in my childish hand, rather than in my now-accustomed cuneiform, was also an unlooked-for foray into—horrors!—regression therapy. I was revisited by a fleeting sense of the novelty and passion that lived in me when the word was still spirit and not yet dull flesh, when it seemed as if there could never be stories enough. It was a cruel glimmer, really, because of course I want it back, I want it back, that unalloyed joy, and of course I can't have it. It's gone for good. The damage is done. It doesn't mattter how much of the library I cast aside, it will always lie buried under the weight of these once and future books.

james merrill

One of the many rude shocks attendant on the death of someone you know well, or to whom you feel deeply connected, is the necessity of being told. There's a kind of implicit insult in this, a suggestion of negligence, as though you've been caught napping. Surely news of such import should reveal itself viscerally at the moment of system shutdown. Surely there shouldn't be any need of brutish words several hours or several days after the fact. "James Merrill died," my partner said to me in a rather offhand aside at dinner the other night.

"Died?"

"I heard it on the radio. In Arizona. A heart attack, I think."

I could scarcely believe it. James Merrill: winner of the National Book Award for poetry, the Pulitzer Prize for poetry, the Bollingen Prize for poetry. James Merrill, whose books I had read and reread, time and again; whose elegant, formal "chronicles of love and loss" (his own words) had given me delight and comfort, and left me slack-jawed with wonder at their virtuoso turns; James Merrill, to whom I had turned more than any other writer for solace and inspiration, who had been part of my life for almost half my tenure on the planet; how could he be dead? Surely I would have known.

I discovered James Merrill by accident during my twenty-second winter. I was at loose ends, newly returned to Winnipeg after a year in France and Italy. I was learning there was some truth to that Wolfe-ian home again, home again dictum. I had loved my time abroad. I had been poor, displaced, and hugely happy in the moment. I had lived in a *garret*, for heaven's sake! I began nursing a raw case of *nostalgie de la boue* within an hour of arriving back in my hometown. Winnipeg! Yeeesh! I felt affronted by its grimy edges and lumpen fashions, diminished by its flat familiarity and untrammelled winds. And that cold season's particular discontent was made all the frostier by troubling questions of sex and sexuality. Winnipeg is not now a hotbed of gay ferment. In 1977, for a shy young man in the throes of coming out, it was a desert.

So, I took comfort in poetry. I wrote it, badly. And I read it, widely. I would go into the public library and harvest the 821 range of the Dewey decimal classification system. I picked volumes off the shelves, indiscriminately, and ploughed through. I read Elizabeth Bishop for the first time, and Philip Larkin, Anne Sexton, Marianne Moore, Wallace Stevens, and W. H. Auden. And most particularly, I read James Merrill. I hadn't heard of him before, although by that time he had published a novel and seven books of poems, and was widely regarded as one of the leading poets of his generation.

I first borrowed a book called *Water Street*, published in 1962, and opened it randomly to "Poem of Summer's End." In a dozen five-line stanzas, it tells of two languid lovers, at the end of an Umbrian summer, taking stock of a long affair. Passion has faded, and a quo vadis question hangs over them. Do they go on together, or take their separate paths? It is a wry and autumnal poem, sad but in no way laden with hopelessness. It has a wistfulness tempered by wit and worldliness that captivated me completely. And although there are no giveaway names or pronouns, and although I knew nothing whatsoever about the poet, I understood instinctively that this was a poem about two men. Subsequently, I would learn that James Merrill was the son of the founder of the Merrill Lynch brokerage; that he was rich beyond telling; that he lived a cosmopolitan life, in New York one week, in Athens the next; and that his partner for many years was a man called David Jackson. But even without such biographical compass points, I was able to discern the tug of homoerotic tension in "Poem of Summer's End" and feel something like relief. After all, what did I know of being gay? My sexual experiences to that point had been cursory and covert, played out over a subtext of shame. I thought I was in for a grim time of it as adulthood took hold. Where could I look to find recorded instances of men who had loved each other deeply and well? Where were the role models through whose example I could formulate a vision of my future? Twenty years ago, in Winnipeg at least, they were not thick on the ground. In *Water Street* and in the James Merrill poems I read subsequently, in *Nights and Days* and *The Fire Screen* and *Braving the Elements*, I found both personal validation and a kind of comfort. Here was a life that was vibrant and fully lived. If such a life was possible, then I might have one too.

I don't want to suggest that my fondness—love, really—for Merrill's writing had its basis only in sociology. I wouldn't have found surcease from sorrow in his books had the poems not been so consistently brilliant: beautifully wrought, artfully constructed, erudite, ironic, mysterious. A 1976 book, *Divine Comedies*, contains a long poem, "The Book of Ephraim," which is the first of a trilogy based on his Ouija board sessions with David Jackson. Over the course of "Ephraim" and the two subsequent volumes (collected in *The Changing Light at Sandover*), an all-star cast of spirits, guides, fleshless eccentrics, intellectuals, and dead poets reveals a funny, complicated, and sometimes maddening cosmology that is both lunatic and convincing. There are not many books of which one can say with confidence: read it and you'll never look at the world in the same way again. This is one.

I always had it in the back of my head that I would write to James Merrill and tell him something of what I've set down here. But of course, I never did. I'm sure I saw him once, in New York, sitting on the steps of the public library, next to the great stone lions that guard the entrance. Of course, I was too timid to make an approach. Now he's dead, and of course, I'm wondering if it's time to excavate my old Ouija board. If the portrait he painted of the great party that is the life beyond this was in any way accurate, there is every possibility that we might yet, somehow, make contact. I might well do this. But not just yet. He'll need to settle in; and anyway, I'm fairly convinced that, for the next couple of weeks at least, his line will always ring busy.

levi anagrams to evil: coincidence?

Thanksgiving is upon us now!
The festive wheels are greased.
A stuffing's been selected and the turkey left to thaw
And clans that span this grandest land are primed to meet and feast,
To mill and swill, to eat their fill, and stuff each gaping maw.

They're primed to now abandon alimentary constraints,
They'll all accrue to rend and chew and overdo, perhaps,
And sure as hell they're primed to knell the usual complaints:
"My God! My gut! My belly! Where's the Bromo? Where's my lap?"

Now I could once be sanguine when I overly indulged.
"Falderal!" I'd gaily call. I knew just what to do:
Some fruit and bran and situps would eliminate that bulge
And I could keep my waist size at a comely 32.

32's the size I've been since I was sweet 16:
4 & 20 years I've been conventionally svelte.
Just last week, however, when I went to buy some jeans
I was forced to change my course and reassess my pelt.

Gentlemen and ladies too, my tale is sad and true.
Hear me say that in the Bay upon a spending spree
Deep within the changing room I shuddered to construe
That somehow now my middle measured—horrors! 33!

It didn't matter how I sucked my gut toward my spine,
Contortions of my portions didn't change things in the least.

Levi's 501s which ought, I thought, to fit me fine
Now were unaccountably at least an inch petite!

"Lord in Heaven, take me now!" I bellowed at the mirror.
Fleshpots, not from Egypt, sagged and could not be confined.
Looking past my shoulder I surveyed my denimed rear.
"Cute" and "pert" were adjectives that didn't come to mind.

This was not the consequence of one expansive binge.
This was something permanent, a gift of middle age.
There and then I thought I might go totally unhinged:
What of Sunday's turkey, stuffed with chestnuts and with sage?

How on earth could I sit down and offer up my thanks,
Eat till overbrimming as I'd often done before
With my waist festooned and ruined by supplementary tanks?
In a trice I saw the light! I bought size 34.

"What the hell," I grumbled as I waddled to the till,
"Now at least I'll freely feast, and freely, too, expand
Sunday night I'll stuff myself from navel unto gills,
And when the host asks "Seconds?" I'll just wave my chubby hand.

poppy

I have this new leather jacket. It's fawn-coloured and smooth, verging on suede, and even though I know it was born of a sentient creature's pain, I wear it guiltlessly. Gleefully, even. I slip my arms through its sleeves of a morning and am filled with the luminous knowing that it looks better on my back than it did when stretched over the spine and ribs of the late cow who first owned it. I have studied myself in it from all angles and in all lights and I can tell you that it is the smartest purchase I ever made. Why, it's nothing short of miraculous! It's just like the enchanted cloak in the fairytales, except that those wraps were mostly used to achieve invisibility, and this dashing bit of haberdashery is appearance-enhancing. Oh, very much so! It makes me look less pallid than is in fact the case. It cinches at the waist, suggesting a svelteness to which I cannot lay claim, and somehow it imparts to my droopy ass (think of a couple of balloons three days after the party) a kind of molded, Chippendale perkiness. When I don the jacket and give the collar a rakish upward flip; when I step out into the world, I walk with an unaccustomed swagger. A devil-may-care, devil-take-the-hindmost swing. Heads swivel. Traffic grinds to a halt. Construction workers up on their booms cease riveting, pucker up, and whistle. Ohhh, baby, baby! You are hot! You are sizzling!

Needless to say, I have come to treat the jacket with a certain tenderness. Reverence, even. I have made it my business to shield it from all harm. So, imagine my horror when the roadside veteran from whom I bought my Remembrance Day poppy decided she would take it upon herself to pin me. Before you could say "Michelangelo's David," she had jabbed the pointy bit right through the unblemished leather. "Did I prick you?" she asked when I yelped. Why, she might as well have shivved me through the aorta! Had she not looked like someone who remembered most of her martial arts training, I might have given her a piece of my mind.

It was an untoward little episode, and it set me to remembering that season or two, back in the early eighties, when I declined either to buy or to wear a poppy. Those were the headily dangerous days of widespread nuclear proliferation, the days of outrage over cruise missile tests at Cold Lake, the days when—on a given Saturday in the spring—tens of thousands of us would wind our way over the Burrard Street bridge and through the downtown to English Bay, singing, chanting, arms linked, righteous, focussed, proud, full of a sense of warm solidarity with demonstrators in Germany and France and Washington, with the brave, cold women camped out on Greenham Common. Somehow, I just couldn't harmonize that action (mild though it was) with sporting one of those felt souvenirs of Flanders over my heart. Those poppies seemed to me then a kind of endorsement, celebratory almost, of those times when the ploughshares were willfully hammered into swords, and all the boys, like lemmings, went off to vent some biologically programmed longing for adventure. Oh, they claimed to be fighting for freedom, but what was that? A diaphanous excuse. An impossible chimera. Poppyless, I made it a point to wear instead buttons emblazoned with pacifist slogans. "What if they gave a war and nobody came?" "In remembrance of every woman raped during every war." And so on. I wonder how many of us have several dozen such badges rattling away in a drawer somewhere.

I know I felt strongly about all this at the time. Now it seems like so much—poppycock. What changed? Just the usual stuff, I guess. Time went by. I aged. I shed some old certainties. Particular hard-line notions were tempered by time, by compromise. Paradoxically, it was observing this dwindling that made me appreciate the power of those youthful, idealistic impulses. It was no longer so easy to be cynical. I was better able to credit the possibility that for the ones who chose to go to war, freedom might actually have been something more than "just another word for nothing left to lose." For all that was awful, for all that was reprehensible, there was also something here to be honoured. History, for one thing. It was the last war that gave the second half of our century its shape. For good or for ill, we can't escape the fact that it made us. It's central to our collective being, and even those of us who were born years after it was over won't stop hungering after its narrative.

"You've never told me about your time in the service," I said to an uncle one night, not so very long ago. We were both at dinner at my parents' home in Winnipeg. I knew he had been in the air force, but had never heard any tales of derring-do.

"No," he said.

Latterly, like so many people of my age, I've become interested in collecting family stories. I pressed for details.

"Where were you stationed? Did you see much action? Were you often in danger?"

He set down his fork.

"Human flesh," he said, "when it burns, smells just like pork."

And that was the story of his war. That was as much as he was willing to tell. I thought how odd it was that his eyes were still clear and blue, in spite of all the unspeakable images that must have passed through those lenses. It's not so hard to figure what he might see when he lowers his lids at night and studies those private screens. I understand the colour of his dreams when I reach for my lovely new jacket and am surprised by the poppy on the left chest. Its silent, bloody mouth. Its still and open heart.

voice mail from hell

"Voice mail from Hell!"
—An office colleague, slamming down her phone in horrified disbelief

Thank you for calling 666-HELL. We in Hell value your business. In order to connect you with the service agent who can most expeditiously handle your inquiry, please pay careful attention to the following instructions. If you are using a rotary phone, either stay on the line or get with the century and buy yourself a touchtone model. You'll have time enough to do that, as well as to shop for a family of six, have your hair coloured, balance your cheque book, and brush up on your Russian in the time it will take us to put your call in a sequencing order, at which point you will know that there are, at a minimum, 500 callers ahead of you, all of whom have questions our one surly receptionist will require an hour or more to answer.

If you are calling from a touchtone phone, like a sensible person, and if you desire service in Latin, press 1 now. For service in English, press pound, then star, then redial, then whistle "Dixie" while punching in the first seven letters of the city of your birth. If you were born in a city the name of which contains fewer than seven letters, such as Regina, you might as well be calling from a rotary phone. Make your language selection now. Thank you.

Use these simple instructions to contact any of the following departments of Hell. For the Legions of the Damned, press 1. For Satan and All His Minions, press 2. For Lucifer and the Fallen Angels, press 3. For Drivers Who Never Turned on Their Left-Turn Signals until They Were Right in the Middle of the Intersection, press 4. For Restaurateurs Who Insisted on Playing the Gypsy Kings, press 5. For Anyone Who Ever Sang "My Way" or "New York, New York" at a Karaoke Bar, press 6. For Die-Hard Liberals and Unrepentant Deviates, press 7. You have pressed 7. Thank you.

If you know the name of the major or minor demon or the damned soul you wish to contact, punch in the first four letters of his or her name now. If not, you will spend what will seem an eternity (and believe us, in Hell we know the meaning of the word) on hold, listening to unbelievably annoying music. For *"Love Is Blue" and Other Memorable Tunes* of Paul Mauriat played on the Hammond organ, very heavy on the vibrato, press 1. For Paul Anka's "Having My Baby" on an endless loop, press 2. For the Barney the Dinosaur rendering of "The Happy Wanderer," artfully blended with a Raffi dance mix, press 3. For Holly Near singing tunes that are near and dear to the hearts of Die-Hard Liberals and Unrepentant Deviates, press 4. You have pressed 4. Thank you.

We are sorry. That selection is unavailable. While you wait for a customer service representative, allow us to tell you about some of the exciting benefits available to our preferred customers through our Frequent Fryer plan. As a Frequent Fryer, you collect points which you can redeem for discounted stays at any one of the stylish hotels, resorts, and museums for which Hell is so widely renowned. Enjoy a relaxing weekend at the Villa of the Slothful or the Palace of the Sodomites! Or take in the Ice Capades, although of course that would only be available on a cold day which is a rare thing in . . .

"Thank you for calling Hell. My name is Oscar. May I help you?"

"Oh, yes! I want to visit the Museum of Covetousness. Can you tell me the opening hours?"

"Would you hold while I look that up?"

(For the next 25 minutes, the Coldstream Guards play the Pachelbel canon.)

"Hello, this is Oscar. I can't seem to find that information. That's Hell for you! I'll transfer you to another agent."

(Sound of clicking, popping, then a ringing. You count 43 ding-a-lings. Then—)

Thank you for calling 666-HELL. We in Hell value your business. In order to connect you . . .

kenn

Truth be told, I don't know why I bother having voice mail. Don't know how I ever got seduced by it. Stupid name. *Voice mail.* Dumb concept, too. Just plain dumb. Trades on the myth of indispensability. *I'm not here, but since we're both of us so terribly important, and since we can neither of us do without the other, and since our lives are so very very chockablock with event, you can leave your message and then I'll leave one for you and then you'll leave one for me and eventually we'll meet by chance in Starbuck's and joke about it and one of us will say "phone tag" and the other will try not to gag.*

Voice mail. Yeeesh. It makes me anxious. You have no control. Everything relies on memory and dexterity. You have to learn which button to push for which function. You have to be deft enough to hit the right one. Most mornings, I can't recollect where my socks are, even if I put them on the night before. Most mornings, I can't load the toaster. It doesn't necessarily get better as the day goes on. With voice mail, a single slip of the finger and everything speeds up, slows down, gets erased, repeats, gets saved for seven days, tells you what time and date the message came in. Tells you how long it is.

Voice mail. All it does is get your hopes up, incite optimism, foster the foolish notion that someone out there is thinking of you. But day after day there are no messages, and so you feel ignored. And when there are messages, they're just from people who want something from you, and so you feel harassed. I mean, I don't know about you, you're reading this on the bus or some damn place, and I can't see you, and you might very well belong to some oppressed group, might have every right to feel ignored and harassed, and if such is the case, believe me, I'm sorry. But as for me, I'm white. I'm middle class. I'm male. I'm employed. The world is my oyster. Oppressed? Harassed? What have I got to complain about? Voice mail? Not fuckin' likely.

Listen, I'm not usually a cranky person. Ask anyone who knows me. Sweet and good-natured and compassionate and kind. These are the adjectives to which they will surely turn to sum me up. But voice mail! That changes everything. It's evil, as I've outlined above. What's more, it can make you try to cheat death. Case in point. Monday, December 18, I get a 37-second message from Kenn. He's inviting me to a solstice party at the end of the week. It's a "drop by if you're in the neighbourhood, if you're free, if you've nothing else planned" kind of message. No urgency. No RSVP required. Even so, common courtesy should have dictated that I phone with my regrets. Especially since it was Christmas. Especially since I only ever saw Kenn twice a year, at the max. Especially since I'd heard through the grapevine that he hadn't been doing very well. I should have called right then and there, like they tell you to do in time management seminars. I should have. But I didn't. I guess I was busy. I guess I meant to get around to it. I guess I just skipped over the message, thinking I'd get to it later in the week. And I should have. But I didn't. I forgot all about the party and the message till it surfaced again in seven days' time, Christmas Day in fact, surfaced along with a warning from the stern time-keeping lady—who's really a computer, don't let her fool you—saying that she would delete Kenn unless I gave her instructions to the contrary. Unless I saved Kenn for another week by pressing 9. Which I did. So that once again I'd be reminded to call, to apologize for my shabbiness. Oh, but it was Christmas week, and I was busy, and I was fretful with my new espresso machine, and I forgot, which was too bad because had I called early enough I might have got him before he went into the hospital. And when his message came up for deletion or renewal in another week's time, on New Year's Day, he was already dead, though I didn't know it, and I remember that I felt a little annoyed with him, irrationally, as I saved his message for a fourth time, wondering how long this would go on.

And now once a week he comes up for renewal, Kenn who died, and it gives me an odd but not unpleasant turn to hear his impossible voice, to think of him setting his sickness to one side to plan his last party, to know that he thought well enough of me to dial my number and talk kindly for 37 seconds while I was away from home, while I was leading my busy little life, while his was winding down. And now, once a week, I press 9 and save him in some digitized drawer of the infernal voice mail machine, save him because I can, because I didn't, because I couldn't, because I might as well, because there's no harm done, because it's little enough to do, now. Save him because he was sweet. Save him because I'm sorry.

umbrella graveyard

I dreamed I found myself in the umbrella graveyard. I stumbled on it unawares; in my dream, I mean. Don't ask whence I came or for where I was bound. Origins and destinations had nothing to do with it; only the here and now were germane in this sleepscape. I looked around. I understood that here was the dark and mournful plain where no tree grows and no bird sings; the mythic and forsaken site where umbrellas that have outlived their usefulness go to die. Their shattered shafts and fractured ribs, of wood and metal. Their tattered membranes, of plastic or silk. Their well-worn handles, some plastic and austere, some ebony and artfully wrought, carved in the shape of pineapples, of parrots. Of skulls. Tawdry, telescoping umbrellas bought at the five-and-dime on an afternoon that turned unexpectedly pluvial and carelessly mislaid hours later, left to malinger on the sticky floor under some cinema seat. No phone calls, no return visits were made in the hope of reclamation, and now they had come to lie here, unmourned, alongside solid, reliable brollies that—after years of dependable service—ran afoul of a gust too strong and herniated on the corner of Granville and Pender. Heirlooms, or something close to it, their casting aside must have precipitated a pang. That sudden shock of loss, of unbreachable absence.

Umbrellas were not a present factor in my "family of origin," as we have learned to say in these times of aggravated sociological sensitivity. They would have been completely out of place in the home where I grew up. We were solid, practical prairie folk who had no need of so whimsical an accessory. That was big sky country. You could see the prosperous banks of clouds long before they arrived to divest themselves of their deposits. And in any case, we could smell the coming rain, learned early on to sniff out its imminence. That was a droughty place, then. Rain was aberrant, easy to forecast, and staying dry became a simple matter of planning to linger indoors. If a downpour went on longer than expected, or if the damp outside became for some unlooked-for reason a necessity, there was sensible gear that could be donned: raincoats, galoshes, and so on. Umbrellas were not unknown, of course. Sometimes they would hove into view, always flowered and dainty models, sheltering either the feyest of girls or else eccentric grannies recently arrived from Manchester. For a man to carry such a sissy contrivance—even a serious black British import—would have been unthinkable. You might just as well have paraded about with a big E, for Emasculation, pinned to your chest.

There was nothing in my rearing or environment to suggest that I would be susceptible to invasion by unsavoury bumbershoot longings. Nonetheless, this happened, and I know at precisely what point I veered off the path, can name the hour and place of contagion. It happened on my ninth birthday, when my parents—the fools! the fools!—took me to see a matinee performance of *Mary Poppins*. It was exactly the wrong thing to do. I was a deeply impressionable nine-year-old, naive in a way that could never be ascribed to today's video-game-playing, media-savvy, Web-surfing children. There in the dark confines of the late and lamented Metropolitan Theatre, when the sun without shone brightly through an atmosphere still thick with undepleted ozone, I fell head over heels in love with Julie Andrews, in love with everything I understood her to stand for. Purity of voice, pertness of personality, precision of accent, a nice turnout in first position, and, mostly, her ability to negotiate the east wind and to fly with an umbrella over the chimneypots and rooftops of Edwardian London. Mine is an August birthday, and I spent the waning days of that hot, dry summer making da Vinci–ish drawings of umbrellas equipped with air jets that would carry me aloft, away to a better place before the snow flew. I think I even dared to ask for an umbrella for Christmas, but the puckered look that passed over the parental face was enough to keep me from insisting too strenuously on such a benefice.

You may not be surprised when I tell you that one of my first purchases when I moved to the West Coast 20 years ago was an umbrella. I felt a heady, self-actualizing joy buying the thing. It was an act of minor rebellion, and whatever residual traces of shame might have surfaced as I approached the counter (think first condom purchase) were mitigated by the certainty that here, such an accoutrement was practically a requirement. It made sense, they were commonplace; I could carry it with impunity, free from the possibility of censure or disapprobation. I remember my delight when I understood that, although I would never be able to use it to counteract the effects of gravity, the umbrella had about it a quality of magic: the way it described a charmed circle and marked out a protected area, a safe zone. A working prayer. Devil rain, don't enter here. Of course, I have long since forgotten what it looked like, that primal umbrella, forgotten where and how I lost it. Had I stumbled over it in the dreamtime graveyard, I don't suppose I would have recognized it, any more than I would have been able to place or name any of the dozens—yes, surely dozens, maybe

even hundreds—of umbrellas that have slipped through my hands
between then and now. The only one I'd have known for sure
would have been the fantasy umbrella from my Julie Andrews–
obsessed childhood, and I suppose I might have looked for it had
I not been jarred awake by the rattling window. An El Nino–
powered wind. The scatter and dash of still more rain.

two sisters, eight legs

I sleep with a man and with two
old nuns. I tell you this just in case you wanted to know. Just in
case you've been wondering, I stand before you and lay this on the
table. The man is thin and smart. He has lots of savvy when it
comes to life management. He goes to bed early, worn out by gar-
dening and *Seinfeld*. He lays his head on the pillow and within
minutes he's as insensible as a weathered, knotty beam. Me, I stay
up late and fret. Sometimes I fret about syntax. Sometimes I fret
about middle age. Neither concern is eased or assuaged by lack of
sleep. The more fool I. It's lonely work, all that fretting. I don't
think I could endure unless I had the two old nuns to keep me company. Sweet nuns! They are fat and devoted. They are steadfast.
They are uncomplaining. Still, I do not envy them their lot. These
two ancient sisters. These round, yawning virgins. These sexless
singers of now and again benisons. Why, imagine! All they do
while I fret the night away is sit nearby, with half-lowered eyes, and
number their beads. They turn over the words of their private
hymns in their hearts. It looks so grim to someone on the outside,
but they will brook no expressions of pity. They know what they're
about, and they know why. They meant it when they took their
vows and embraced their particular mission, even though it
involves next to nothing in material compensation. Which is fine
with them. They care nothing for such things. They have no possessions other than the simple effects they carried in on their backs
when they arrived here as novitiates. That was a long time ago.
Between them, they can lay claim to eight legs, two tails, and 20
years. Nothing more.

At first glance, you wouldn't necessarily guess they have embraced the religious life. They don't look like everyday sisters. One nun has copper eyes and wears a habit that is unremittingly black. The other nun's vestment is off-white. She has floppy ears and a beard. The black nun is wholly cloistered, but not committed to silence. She serves her vocation by watching and singing. What she knows of the earth she has learned by way of windows. She watches the starlings building a nest in the next-door eaves and praises the Lord enthusiastically for His wisdom in making such fascinating creatures. She is sure that the All-Knowing, All-Seeing One even thought to make them delicious. Not that she hungers after something so worldly. When a cat comes through the garden, her nunnish tail triples in width and she breaks into intricate anthems, the sense of which I can never discern. I think they may be in Latin. *Hodie*, I think she sometimes squawks. *Hodie, hodie.* Her only concern is to draw attention to the wonders of Creation. Sometimes, she is moved to hurl herself percussively against the glass, or to hang from the screen by her claws. *Christus natus est!* she calls, her heart nearly exploding with rapture. The white nun's work requires she move about in the world at least three times a day. In order that she not be taken in by its temptations, she only goes out on the end of a leather tether. Her mission on these dangerous forays is to look for pieces of the one true cross. She is forever thinking she has found one and lunging after it, although it more often than not turns out to be a chicken bone maliciously impersonating a relic.

Dear old nuns. I don't know what I'd do without them. They work in subtle ways to keep me sane. Shortly after midnight, they nudge me off to the bed where the thin man already lies. I slide in beside him. The white nun takes to her basket. The black nun spreads my legs and lies in the heat of the one true crotch. I set my fretting aside. I welcome sleep in. The nuns continue to say their prayers, to make their interventions, to ask for proofs of God's love for me, a backward slider. It works, too. Sometimes in the morning I will wake and see that something has changed. Perhaps, as happened recently, my chest hair will have turned white. Perhaps, as happened not long ago, I will awake full of the burning desire to take up curling, something that could only occur through the most vigorous divine intervention. Just the other day I looked at the calendar before going out the door to work and understood, deep in my heart, that it was now safe to plant fragile annuals. Sometimes a troublesome sentence will write itself across the back of my lids just before I open my eyes. Sometimes I will feel young again. It's nothing, it's nothing, say the two fat nuns. It's nothing more than love. And they stretch. And they yawn. The thin man is already in the shower. It's time to go on.

visit twice a year for a beautiful smile

The World Federation Dental Conference is taking place in Vancouver this October. Fourteen thousand dentists will forsake their dams and drills and gather to discuss periodontal techniques and compare Rolexes.

I learned this news the same day I read there will be a congress of cowboys gathering in September at the old O'Keefe Ranch, near Vernon. Now, as in days of yore, chaps who wear chaps are enthusiastic poets; and one of the highlights of the cowboy assembly will be a presentation of this folksy oeuvre.

Why is it that chasing dogies out where the deer and the antelope play awakens a poetic instinct, while labouring over plaque and delivering stern warnings about the dangers of gingivitis does not? I can't imagine that there is any real impediment to dentists stripping off their latex gloves and trying their hand at scribbling a verse or two. I think perhaps it just hasn't occurred to them, as a profession, that such a thing might enhance their public image. So, by way of encouragement, I offer up the following examples of what dental poetry might look like. This first instance reflects deep pride in the profession; the same deep pride that sings through so clearly in the lines written by cowboys.

> Folks who work in offices are desk-bound all day long.
> Other folks can work outside and hear the robin's song.
> Some folks work when shines the sun, and some when lamps are lit.

I thank the lord the work I do involves a lot of spit.
I thank the lord, I shout hurrah, I say, "Strike up the band!"
Each time I see the evidence of salivary glands.
I start to shake and tremble, get all flustered, feel a fool,
Each and every time I see a patient start to drool.
When the day is over I can hardly help but fidget,
Waiting till the morning comes and I can soak my digits.
Quaker, Jew or Anglican, or Seventh Day Adventist,
It's a strange pathology but that's why I'm a dentist.
Yeehaw!

Cowboy poetry often has a spiritual aspect to it, a keen awareness of how those who ride the range are at one with the turf and the sky and the saddle and the cows and the hills and the stars and the coyotes and the beans and so on. Dental poetry would surely betray this same cosmic sensitivity.

Just as sure as north is on the other side of south,
I can always find a world, entire, in every mouth.
Rounder than the girdled globe, and peopled up and down:
Every common molar, like a king, deserves a crown,
Every sweet bicuspid, each incisor, and each gum:
Take them all together, they are happiness' sum.
Yahoo!

And finally, every cowboy has a "git along little dogie" song to sing to his horse. Why shouldn't dentists have a jaunty verse to chant as they slide into their BMWs and head out to work?

Get along, little Flossy, though the office is far
I know that we'll get there, you're a hot German car.
You're a pricey convertible, and your top's down,
Get along, little Flossy, get along into town.
Singing No-vo-cain, get along, little Flossy,
Get along, little Flossy, though long is the haul.
Singing No-vo-cain, get along, little Flossy,
We've got bridges to cross, and a few to install.
Yeee-ooooowwwww!

By gum! The more I think of this the more I like it. A folk art is waiting. Perhaps it's not too late to schedule a workshop at the dentists' meeting. All that would be needed would be a facilitator and two or more to gather in his name. My own schedule in October is clear. And I barter! Wanna swap a rhyme for "orthodontia" for a filling?

necessary occlusions

I saw my boyfriend, Philip, from the window. He was arriving home from his twice-yearly excursion into caries detection and plaque removal. He walked up the street with the self-assured swagger of one who's been X-rayed and found blameless. He came through the door flashing choppers so glistening they could blind you if the light was right. He also bore a discreet spool of floss (bubblegum-flavoured, which is both recent and revolting), a talented new toothbrush with a gift for reaching hard-to-clean places, and the interesting news that his dentist had a favour to ask of me.

I was surprised, but also not. It would never occur to me to enter with a dentist into the pact-making intimacy that is the foundation for this kind of once-removed favour-asking. However, it was plain from the beginning that Philip would forge a special bond with his beloved Dr. Cinderella Varislovsky. After their first session he had told me with frank admiration of how, in her native Leningrad—or whatever it's called now—she was a neurosurgeon. She turned to dentistry when our sticky health-care regulators wouldn't recognize her qualifications after she landed as a refugee on these shores almost 20 years ago.

"But surely it would have taken her less time to get relicensed as a neurosurgeon than it would to become a dentist," I suggested, with the nit-picking Cartesian coolness which is so much a part of me, and which has ruined a great many stories.

"No doubt. But she wanted a whole fresh start. A new country. A new job. A new life."

"Ah."

Although I couldn't dispute that there was a kind of emotional logic operative in this scenario, I was nonetheless troubled by an evident imbalance in the narrative. I mean that her transfer of vocational affection seemed so much less far-flung than the geographic shift she had endured. I couldn't help but think that were I a neurosurgeon hankering after a major career change—but still wanting to preserve some medical underpinnings—I'd have given serious thought to becoming, say, a podiatrist. Shouldn't simple prudence have dictated such a measure? After all, one of the distinguishing marks of the mouth is its close proximity to the brain. Might she not risk being invaded, in unforeseen and delicate moments, by that terrible, gnawing nostalgia to which the Slavic races are notoriously susceptible? What if, in an episode of profound and nameless hunger, she rammed a drill or pick or one of the other sharp objects to which she would have access up through the roof of a patient's mouth, just to revisit her old stomping grounds?

No eventuality is too strange to imagine, and I say this with some certainty. I am in my forties now, and there is little I haven't seen or at least heard of. Even so, I spared Philip a recitation of the litany of my fears. In his most charitable mood he would dismiss them as far-fetched. He might also get quite riled, since he is someone who needs heroes in his life. Over the years I have learned that I malign his chosen idols—of whom Dr. Varislovsky is one—at my peril.

"A favour?" I asked as he attached the six-months-hence appointment reminder card to the fridge with a nifty red pepper magnet. On the door of our Inglis, fruits and vegetables vie for space with tiny, lavender-coloured chips on which are written words that are meant to be of interest to homosexuals. These faggy parts of speech were last year's Yuletide token from my best friend, Bonnie. They are not, I have to say, up to her usual standard of gift-giving. When I opened them I could almost smell the grade-B card shop where they'd languished on the shelf until she snatched them up two minutes before closing time on Christmas Eve. But perhaps I'm being too harsh. They are not utterly bereft of charm. It is possible to enter a state of meditative calm while arranging them into a delicate haiku or any other cryptic maxim. Angelina, our cleaning lady, takes care to rearrange them each and every week.

Closet Dyke So Cute
Campy Boy Has Beautiful Body
Hot Leather Daddy 69 With Me

I freely admit I looked at Angelina with an invigorated regard after she began leaving such snippets in her sparkling wake, along with her requests that we replenish the supply of Vim.

"4 p.m., May 17" was the rather more mundane message on the appointment card Philip affixed to the fridge door adjacent to the word "Suck." The backward slant favoured by Cinderella's receptionist sang out with succinct and cheerful optimism. A prophecy. A dumb assurance.

"What sort of favour? Is she after a cut rate on a ballroom?"

I asked this not because I was poking fun at her Christian name—which had been Valentina in her motherland and which she had changed on a *nouveau monde* whim—but because I supposed that Cinderella was planning a meeting for her professional association and wanted me to pull some work-related strings. I'm a freelance convention organizer with ace connections to all the big downtown hotels. The day doesn't go by that some forgotten school chum or vague associate from days of yore doesn't call up on behalf of a group representing teachers, accountants, social workers, mechanical engineers, you name it, and try to weasel something out of me for next to nothing.

"Dr. Varislovsky thinks I grind my teeth at night."

"I've never heard you."

"You wouldn't wake up if I tried to gnaw your arm off."

This was true enough. Sleeping soundly is one of my few gifts. Legion are the anecdotes concerning the events and situations I've dozed through. Some are apocryphal. Others are not. Should I ever have the chance to meet Luciano Pavarotti, I will apologize to him for snoring during his rendering of "Nessun Dorma."

"So?"

"So, she thought you might not mind staying awake some night."

"Awake?"

"To listen. To see whether I do or don't."

"What?"

"Grind. It tends to happen in the rem stage, which means you'd have to stay on the lookout for two hours after I dropped off. And then we'd know."

"About the grinding."

"Exactly."

"Does it have to be tonight? I'm kind of tired."

"Whenever."

"Well. Maybe. We'll see."

My degree is in art history. All I know of scientific protocols I learned in grade 10 biology, a course I nearly failed for questioning our teacher's certitude that the frogs we were pinning down and unseaming from nave to chops had no feelings. This is a concept I now apply quite easily to lawyers, but at the age of 15 I passionately refused to believe it was so of amphibians. Of course, that was years and years ago, and I've long since forgotten everything I might have learned. All the same, the specific vocabulary of that place and time kept coming back to me as I contemplated my eventual vigil. It seemed to me there were flaws in the basic hypothesis that were going to make such an inconvenience a necessity. I wanted to visit the good doctor in her office and ask impertinent and penetrating questions about the scientific method, about controlled experiments, about necessary proofs. So much seemed to be riding on Cinderella's linking of the most diaphanous of assumptions: that teeth were being ground at all, that it was bound to happen at a particular stage of sleep, that it happened each and every time Philip nodded off, and that therefore I would be able to detect it on the random night I stayed awake, and so on and so forth. These were the minor cavils that leaped to mind, and that I held myself back from voicing just for the sake of keeping peace in our house.

"I wouldn't be at all surprised," Bonnie said when she called me up the next morning and I told her why a Russian whose personal acquaintance I had yet to make had asked me to sign up for the graveyard shift on grind patrol. It was after 10, but I was still quite woozy; for though I'd made no effort to comply with the nervy Cinderella's outré demand, my sleep had nonetheless been troubled by dreams of molars marching like Brown Shirts, their jackboots sparking on the pavement. I would wake with a start, time and again. I'd listen in the dark for the telltale sound of enamel on enamel but hear nothing other than slow breathing and, once, the freep of a fart.

"Nope. It wouldn't surprise me in the slightest to learn that he's a nocturnal clencher. It would explain the tight-jawed look he favours."

Bonnie's lighter clicked as she fired up what would be her sixth or seventh smoke of the day. She was calling from the house in which she'd grown up, the very house where her mother was presently installed and taking her time with the business of dying. I imagined my Bonnie, who was lying not over the ocean but just across False Creek, leaning out the ancestral kitchen window, exhaling insubstantial Christmas wreaths into the damp December air. Bonnie had never been tempted by cigarettes until the day her mother was diagnosed with lung cancer, at which point she took up smoking with a vengeance. Bonnie calls it "a defiant irony." I see it as a way of venting rage. Philip thinks she's out of her mind.

There is little love lost between my best friend and my boyfriend, which is not the most convenient of situations. I'll spare you the specifics, the whys and the wherefores. Suffice it to say that Bonnie thinks Philip is stuffy and retentive and insufferable. Philip thinks Bonnie is immoral and opportunistic and terribly indiscreet. In fact, the one request he made of me when his blood work came back from the lab with the unsettling word "positive" attached to it was that I say nothing to Bonnie. She makes film documentaries and has a project underway that involves following the progress— if that is the word—of several HIV patients. Philip felt sure she would pressure me to pressure him to allow her access to his days. This prospect made his bile freeze in its ducts.

"The last thing I want," he said, with the intractable ire that is so particular to the outraged taxpayer, "is for the Canada Council to support the chronicling of my slow decline."

So far, I have adhered to his request. I've kept my counsel, even though I sometimes feel as if I'm swelling up with other people's illness, which can hardly be healthy. Sometimes, I think I might explode.

"How's your mom?" I asked my chief gal pal, holding the phone to my ear with my shoulder in exactly the posture the chiropractor warned me against, all the while dicking around with some words on the fridge.

Queer Rights Are Fabulous
Oh You Sexy Lover

"She's holding. That's about the best that could be said of it. I think she's determined to ruin one last Christmas."

Her voice was broken by what I took to be emotion but what proved in fact to be the discreet belch that signals another caller clamouring for attention. It was a well-respected virologist calling from Dallas and wanting to have a long and serious talk about the canapés I was arranging for the opening-night reception of yet another upcoming international AIDS confab.

"Call me tonight," she said as I rang off and geared myself up to sing hymns to Mr. Texas about the glories of our local wines and the reasonable price of cream cheese and the fabulous group rate at the posh hotel where the conferees would gather in the spring: the very hotel where, as it happens, the first person I ever knew who died of what the more forthright obituaries call "AIDS-related causes" worked as a night clerk.

Brandon. That was his name. He said his parents named him Brandon because that was where they went on their honeymoon and that was where he had been conceived. I thought he was joking, mostly because I worked in a group home in Brandon one summer when I was still at school, and while it's a nice enough place, very clean and all, and there are some terrific lawns, no one would ever mistake it for Niagara Falls.

I met his folks at his funeral. They told me all in a rush that it was their first trip ever outside of Manitoba, their first time to Vancouver, and they had come to bury their son whom they had never visited when he was ill, but how could they have known because he'd never told them anything was wrong, had never mentioned this cancer of his, and had he suffered at the end? I remembered his story about his naming, which I had never believed to be a literal truth but which now I saw was that very thing, and I was filled with wonder at the idea of those two sweet people lying together and weeping with the joy of their first night together, never thinking their experimental probings were going to bear such fruit, such pain, such loss. It broke my heart to see their confusion.

Brandon found religion in his declining days, reverting to the Catholicism he had renounced in his youth along with so much else. "Is there anything I can do for you?" I asked him once, thinking I might be able to fetch him some magazines or help him make some phone calls.

"Pray for me."

His voice was so weak I had to make him repeat himself half a dozen times before I understood.

"Sure," I answered, for no other answer would have served and I found myself in the enviable position of being the one who had absolutely nothing to lose.

Here is a question I sometimes ask myself, and which I might be tempted to spell out on our fridge if I had sufficient words. What can we do, in these perilous times, to lead honourable lives? Remove the labels from tins and bottles before we put them in the blue box for recycling. Pay the Airport Improvement Fee without complaining. Refrain from smoking pipes and cigars for the comfort of other patrons. Turn off cel phones, beepers, and watch alarms before a concert begins. All these things can we undertake. Perhaps there is also something to be said for honouring our promises, even the dumb and lavish ones. Which is why I keep Bonnie in the dark. Which is why I rerouted myself on my way home from the hospital and pulled into the deserted parking lot of a Catholic holy place. I suppose I could have prayed as easily in my living room, or in the express line at the Safeway, but this church-stopping instilled in me the feeling that I was going straight to the source. It was not the institution that had nurtured my own stunted sense of spirituality, but the outright purity of my purpose in entering there made me feel less like a clumsy intruder or interloper or infidel than I might have done, had I just gone in to gawk at a few icons or write an investigative piece about priests and orphaned altar boys.

I took my time about my business, trying to call to mind the antique rituals I'd observed in such helpful movies as *The Trouble with Angels* and *The Nun's Story* while I went through my prayerful paces. I deposited a loonie in a box near the door, heard it clunk satisfactorily against the coins of the truly faithful. I selected a taper from a waxy pile, lit it, and added it to the ranks of the several candles that already burned there, unattended even though they leaned wonkily and perilously into one another. Then I walked up the aisle, turning churchy words over in my mind. Narthex. Transept. Nave. Monstrance. Sacristy. Vestry. Host. I moved slowly and with some small pomp, bridelike, and executed a little curtsy before the altar. It was around this point that I began to feel I was running the risk of committing procedural gaffes.

Relieved that I was alone and unobserved, I squeezed into a pew and surveyed the visible statuary. There were various saints and angels. There was Jesus, hanging dependably and reassuringly on his cross. There was Mary, white alabaster, looking down from a less treacherous perch. She was a picture of calm, turning over the centuries in her stony heart. Under her decorous gaze, I lowered my head and began to pray. It surprised me to find that I moved my lips and that such arcane and archaic vocabulary came so easily to my mind.

"Blessed Mary, Mother of God, smile on us sinners and show us your grace. Remember your servant Brandon, and comfort him in this his hour of need. Shine Thy light upon him . . ."

Perhaps it was forming the unfamiliar word "thy" with my mouth that made me swallow a half-chewed snicker and look up just as a trickle of blood, a sticky, crimson rivulet, dribbled from the usually blameless button of the Virgin's nose. There was a physical shifting in the room. The air went all hot and electric, the way it will when lightning strikes too close for comfort, or when an old lover calls after a prolonged silence. An unaccustomed current coursed up my spine, as though some kind of universal power source had plugged itself into my central nervous system. I have never felt so powerful, so all-knowing. The trinity, transubstantiation, immaculate conception, differential calculus, the Edict of Nantes, what Quebec wants: the deeper truths of all these mysteries were available to me. I could have asked for anything in the world and it would have been mine. The winning numbers to every future 649, a frost-free fridge with an ice-maker, a house in the country, peace on earth, any cure for any illness. Had I simply had the wit to say the words, Bonnie's mother would be in training for the marathon and Philip would be paying close attention to RRSP options. Unfortunately, I gave in to an urge to sneeze, and when I opened my eyes a split second later and looked around, Mary's face was without blemish and Brandon was dead, although I didn't know it until the next day when I called in with some flowers and a month's worth of *Maclean's*.

I never told my boyfriend about my close brush with omnipotence. I came close a few months back, though. It was when the television was spilling pictures of delighted Hindus all over the world, gathering in their temples to marvel at how their elephant statues were swilling milk. "Oh, Jesus," sneered Philip when a respected physicist in Bombay or Toronto or somewhere claimed that he, too, had seen this miracle with his very eyes. Philip picked up the remote and changed channels with a secular bravado I found offensive. I thought it wouldn't hurt to tell him that the world is not as straightforward and rational a place as it seems. I thought it wouldn't hurt for him to know that the man he was pleased to call his lover once came perilously close to being fricasseed by an encounter with the Lord. And while I was at it, I thought I might just ask the bastard if he cared to tell me how the hell he got infected in the first place since my own blood might as well be white, it runs so clean. I'm glad I held back, however. It was not the moment to raise such far-reaching fancies and queries. His counts were down ever so slightly for the first time. Even though he was still healthy as a horse, I half-imagined I could see a translucency to his skin and the outline of his skull showing through.

That was in the summer. The dark days are on us now, and that's for sure. Over the Burrard Street Bridge, Bonnie's mother is gasping her last. And the man who lies beside me at night has a time bomb that is passed from cell to cell in his secret blood. My own circumstances are also, momentarily, reduced. I am writing this by flashlight beam, lying supine in the empty tub in our en suite bathroom. The door is open to the bedroom, where Philip has been sawing a log for over an hour now. Tonight is the night for which Cinderella has hoped and prayed lo these several weeks. Positioned where and as I am, I'm sure to hear the dreadful gnashing, if and when it kicks in. It's bloody uncomfortable, but at least the bathtub is glistening, as the thorough Angelina was here today. I can only suppose that the festive season has instilled in her an uncommonly savoury mood. "Make A Wish" were the pleasant, innocuous words she arranged on the fridge door. I've done that. It was a modest plea. I wished for only this wakefulness, which is enough to ask of a universe beleaguered by other people's tragedies and requirements. I wished only that I might stay alert while my cantankerous man's rem eyeballs do their pinball shuffle under his shadowy lids. While he dreams, I'll listen for his incisors to collide. Or not. Whatever the case may be. I have no idea what news he really wants to hear. After all, there is a certain romance to pathology. For all I know, in his heart of hearts, he's looking forward to visiting Cinderella wearing a hangdog, why-me look and having her fuss over him while she engineers his mouth guard or other orthodontic device. Come the morning, I'll bring him the *Globe and Mail* and his coffee in his favourite "I ♥ New York" mug. I'll kiss his scratchy, whiskered cheek. I'll sit beside him on the bed and tell him the truth as I have come to understand it. And then we'll both just have to live with it.

101 damnations

Angel of Perversity settled on my shoulder. Settled there Christmas Day. Christmas Day, no less! Settled there and whispered in my ear. Whispered, "Go see *101 Dalmatians*." *101 Dalmatians*? Something I'd have never thought of for myself. Bad combination! *101 Dalmatians* and Christmas Day! Yeeeee! All those kids! All those parents! All that evidence of loathsome vogue for remaking, retouching, reissuing everything from sixties, from seventies! Songs, movies, books, whatever. Why? No one has any new ideas? Nostalgic boomers eager to maintain cultural hegemony? Wasn't good enough first time round? As if! Feel especially strong about *101 Dalmatians* in this regard. *101 Dalmatians* = Sacred Work of Art. *101 Dalmatians* = First Movie I Ever Saw. The original, that is. The cartoon. Something like 35 years ago. (Hurts to write that down. 35 years. Ouch.) Pivotal moment in intellectual development. Fell in love with movies. Fell in love with Cruella. Stored away in brain in file marked, "Icons, Camp, Lesbian—Future Reference." Had no longing to see Glenn Close try to make Cruella flesh. None. But Angel of Perversity settled on my shoulder. Said go. Couldn't refuse. "No" not in vocab of A.O.P. So, headed out. Headed out full of nostalgia and trepidation.

Found theatre. Found theatre full of kids. Found seat in theatre full of kids. Kid behind kept kicking back of chair. Kicking back of chair and whining, "When we gonna get 101 Damnations? When we gonna get 101 Damnations?" Should have been annoyed. Should have waxed snide. Should have turned around and advised accompanying parent on birth control techniques in order to avoid future unhappiness. Instead, was suddenly filled with deep sense of peace. Of mission. Of purpose. Miraculous! 101 Damnations! *Quel* concept! Exactly what world needs! After all! Consider! Dreadful paucity of good curses in the land! Yet so many situations when imprecations might come in handy! Pity! No one left on planet possessed of biblical sense of occasion! No one able to hold forth with Mosaic flourish, as in Deuteronomy: "Cursed shall be thy basket and thy store. Cursed shall be the fruit of thy body and the fruit of thy land, the increase of thy kine, and the flocks of thy sheep." So very tiresome, resorting always to, "Yo! Dickhead!" Crude! Ugly! Limiting! 101 Damnations! A.O.P. on shoulder whispered in ear. Whispered, "Start!" Found used popcorn container. Found pen. Began to compose *101 Damnations: Contemporary Curses for Unsavoury Situations*. Got four done before movie started. Here goes.

1. *At the laundromat: dryer trap thick with lint*
   Matted dross of underwear,
   Fleece bound up with curly hair,
   Shirty remnants, bits of socks,
   Residue of sweaty jocks:
   He who left you lives in sin!
   In Hell's dryer may he spin!

2. *At the dinner table: guest waits till seated to announce his dietary restrictions*
   Now let me be quite certain that I fully understand:
   You're veggie, so that means you won't, of course, ingest the
       lamb.
   You won't be having soup because you can't abide the cream,
   And bread is out as wheat engenders problems with the spleen.
   The peas are not organic, so I'll tell you what we'll do.
   Since you're so damn free-range, my friend, we'll just tuck
       into you.

3. *In the elevator: cougher hacks violently*
   Phlegmy, raspy Queen of Sputum
   Spew not on my Aquascutum.
   Holding tank of noxious gasses,

Dot not my Armani glasses.
Pray confine your viral spraying,
Likewise stem your nasal braying.
We know how to make you stable:
Lock you in and cut the cable.

4. *In bed: wide awake in the wee hours*
Oh waiter, dear waiter, wherever you are,
I hope that your eyes are shut tight,
For mine are wide open. I take in the stars,
For sleep is a stranger tonight.
You said it was decaf, I said "Bring it on!"
You ferried me cup after cup.
It's five in the morning and verging on dawn,
And waiter I find I'm still up.
I start work at seven, so now I'm inspired
To think of you coming to harm.
I'm hoping there might be a three-alarm fire,
And you'll slumber through the alarm.

in the madding crowd

Welcome, Yule! Once again you dwell among us, your kit bag brimming with the incompatible impulses and contradictory emotions with which the season is freighted. Now we can count on seeing conventionally mature men and women transformed into regular catherine wheels, brightening the air around them with sparks of childlike enthusiasm. They cannot keep so much good cheer, so much love, to themselves, and when they meet another who scatters those same hot sparks in equal measure, they will each play moth to the other's flame. A Christmas romance—who has not witnessed such a blossoming and burning?

Conversely, we will see once-fiery couples, who have held each other hostage for years, now unable to kindle even an ember of enthusiasm for one another or for the festive imperatives December brings. They will admit that they are past all annealing and have come undone. A Christmas split-up—who has not been through one?

And as we honour the timeless myth of miraculous birth, we will see how ailing old people willfully sicken and die, slipping away a day or two before Christmas, unable to endure the inevitable racket and fuss; or perhaps they'll stop their ears against Death's importuning, will linger to enjoy one last family get-together and achieve some kind of clannish gestalt before taking permanent leave on Boxing Day. A Christmas death—who cannot imagine having one, sooner or later?

Bucko! you say. Cheer up! Outside the snow is falling and friends are calling yoo-hoo! Why assail us with such subfusc sobriety? As always, I blame it on my souvenirs. Recently, having fallen prey to a tidying impulse, I took some time to sort through the dross of the last several years. In an unmarked box full of miscellaneous crap, I found a couple of those one-use-only, disposable cameras. Each of their 24 exposures had been claimed, though for what purpose and on which occasions I had no notion or recollection. Curiosity got the better of me, and rather than doing the sensible thing—which would have been to take a cue from the word "disposable"—I dropped them off for developing. When I retrieved the photos several days later, they proved to be snaps of a Christmas party I'd given in, I think, 1992. Ah! Of course! It all came back. Those cameras! I had left them out so that my guests could take random shots of the merriment as it unfolded. I'd once been at a wedding where this was done, to famous effect. And now, half a decade later, here they were, about 40 of the 48 images discernible.

At the end of *Slaves of New York*, the Merchant Ivory adaptation of the collection of stories by Tama Janowitz, Eleanor—an insecure maker of fanciful hats who has finally managed to dump her philandering boyfriend—holds a big party. When one of her guests asks her why she has chosen to do such a thing (a good question not often enough asked of party-givers) she answers—and here I paraphrase—that she did it to acknowledge, in a public way, the possibility of happiness, as well as to assert selfhood. By assembling a bunch of convivial people around her, she proved she could be her own glad person in the middle of a madding crowd.

I remember this because I saw *Slaves of New York* a night or two after giving my own party, and I was struck by an "Eleanor, *c'est moi*" dawning. After enduring several big life changes of the usual kinds, I was beginning to know myself again. I needed to do something to mark the new phase, to mark my reemergence. A party, of course! The perfect gesture! To forestall the possibility that no one would turn up, I issued what must have been hundreds of summonses. I invited everyone I knew socially and collegially, invited everyone in the building in which I lived, invited people to whom I hadn't spoken in years, people I met at the bus stop, invited strangers who stopped and asked for directions to the Pacific Centre mall. And over the course of the night, literally hundreds of people, including an alarming number of the strangers, put in an appearance. When the oxygen was depleted in the apartment, the party spilled into the hallway. At a given point, when I couldn't stand it any more, I took to riding the elevator up and down just to get away from the noise and the shouting and the laughing; just to escape the crowd I'd caused to assemble, none of whom guessed, I don't suppose, that they were there because I was acting out a particular dysfunction. The next day, I removed 150 empty wine bottles to the recycling bin down the alley.

A good time was had by many, to judge from these pictures. Arms are linked, faces are flushed, there are many goofy smiles. And look, here are two people who met that night, who fell in love and are still a unit. They are having what might be their first conversation. Here is a couple who dissolved their relationship just a few weeks later, smiling and looking relaxed in spite of whatever tensions they might have been experiencing domestically. No one would have guessed they were about to unravel. And here is a young man who's dead now. And here's another. And another. And still one more. Four? Yes, at least four. Five years ago it was, and they knew they weren't far from their endings. We all knew. We could see it in the pale masks of their faces. Even so, they smiled. And here they are again, after all those years of confinement; once more among us, the lives of this and many other parties, come to sadden us, to gladden us with the proof that they were here, and they were happy, and now they're gone. It's a rotten time of year for missing people, but really, what else can you do? Just kiss them, here and here, and send them on their way. God rest you merry, gentlemen. Let nothing you dismay.

shopping for god

We've reached again the time of
year when angels, heard on high,
Gather in celestial fields to strum their pale guitars.
And skate across the milky spill that spans the frozen sky,
And strew their silky tinsel, strand by strand, on silver stars.

They get each other presents, too: bright haloes, combs for wings,
And tennis shoes—for thus, I've heard, are angels these days shod.
And also harp accessories—the tuning forks, the strings
And each and every one of them buys something nice for God.

This isn't problematic, as at first it surely seems.
You'd be quite right in thinking that there's nothing he requires.
He doesn't need a journal to record his lucid dreams,
He doesn't need a toolbox full of drill bits, screws, and pliers.

Whatever do you give someone who, after all, devised
The world in half a dozen days and didn't break a sweat?
A bottle of cologne is hardly apt, and nor are ties.
He has a great sufficiency of all there is to get.

But nonetheless a gesture is required, and so the bands
Of winged and perfect angels to his mansion beat a path,
All bearing one of two gifts in their insubstantial hands:
Bonbons for his bedside, or else bubbles for his bath.

Yes, God likes nothing better than to linger in the tub,
Immersed in frothy bubbles. Too divine! Oh, purest bliss!
He'd rather far eat chocolate bars than any other grub:
And this explains his fondness for the Belgians and the Swiss.

He greets the angels as they come and calls them by their names.
He chortles, "Welcome, welcome," and embraces them with care.
For if he hugs them heartily, they might well come up lame:
Angels, after all, are made of wishes, light, and air.

He ladles out the eggnog first: it's thick and laced with rum,
Or else there is a fruity punch for those who don't indulge.
Everyone eats angel cake till he or she grows numb,
And jokes abound about the coming battle of the bulge.

He opens presents reverently, the wrap he folds and stows.
"Waste not, want not," is his motto. God is famed for thrift.
How he will react is no surprise. Each angel knows
He'll trill "My very favourite!" when he opens every gift.

Boxes full of chocolates soon are stacked beside his throne,
Bottles full of bubble bath are added to the pile.
Soon enough his guests will go and he'll be home alone,
And though he likes their company, the prospect makes him smile.

The angels tell the boss good-bye. He bids them all good cheer.
He says, as he's obliged to, "Must you go? Oh, can't you stay?"
He has supplies to last him now throughout the coming year.
He waves and watches fondly as they scamper on their way.

"How do you know that this is so?" I hear the doubters bark.
To which I'll say without delay, "I made it up, of course!"
So don't take down your testaments to prove me off the mark.
Imagination paired with observation is my source.

For there are days when I look up and see the spinning clouds—
The cumulus accumulate, the nimble nimbus froth—
And I declare that way up there, remote from mortal crowds,
I have witnessed God supine reclining in the bath.

And furthermore if we explore the rainbow's graceful bend,
It's plain that light and physics can't explain those gentle hues.
It's God dismantling chocolate creams the angels thought to send,
Spilling liquid centres while he thinks which one to choose.

Theologists will say that my cosmology is flawed,
And physicists will tell you I am sadly out of joint:
They would put a different face on science and on God.
Before I cede the podium, I'll make my final point.

If there is a Creator, and I rather think there is,
Who made us in his image, every woman, child, and man,
Then things which give us pleasure must be pleasures, too, of his,
Unless we've lost entirely our primal master plan.

So with this syllogism then, we reach my fable's end:
Pleasure is a godly thing, and one of life's rewards.
Quibble if you have to, but I cling to this, my friend:
Bubble baths and bonbons bring us closer to our Lord.

double snackers

For some reason, probably related
to the onset of middle age, I've been hankering after the foods I
loved as a child. Last week in Winnipeg, I spent a happy Sunday
afternoon thumbing through my mother's cookbooks, searching
out the recipes for her famous sandwich spread, her chocolate chip
cookies, and her matchless mustard sauce. Most of their various
whys and wherefores are recorded in her several church cookbooks: books she either assisted in compiling or that came her way
via neighbours or aunties or rummage sales.

My favourite of these was assembled 60 years ago by the
women's committee of St. Stephen's Broadway United Church. This
fragile artifact from the 1930s contains reliable directions for feeding a hundred: 15 pounds boiled boneless ham, 100 ribs of beef
(raw), and 50 spring chickens. The women's committee also managed to coax from Miss K. Halliday the secret of her Nice Drink for
Hot Days. Mrs. Ray lifts the veil on her Egg Shampoo for Hair.

There are winning endorsements from sponsors, too. MacDon-
ald's Shoe Store ("You are as young as your feet") advises that "The
Best Cook Will Cook with Comfortable Feet." The Manitoba Telephone System recommends the acquisition of a home telephone,
which "is more than a convenience and a social asset. It is also a
protection in emergencies, a means of securing bargains, and it
enables you to avoid going out in weather which is ruinous to
clothes and hazardous to health." I found myself charmed by all

this, almost against my will; charmed by what I took to be the evidence of a simpler, easier time not so far distant from our own. I know full well that this is illusory; that the congregants of St. Stephen's Broadway were prey to the same lusts, hungers, and disappointments that plague us today; that their children died more readily and dreadfully than is now the case; that they had seen one appalling war and were about to see another. Even so, I was inhabited by a longing for a time when "getting on line" meant signing up for a five-digit telephone number.

Here and there, interspersed between the leaves of the book, were recipe cards, mostly inscribed in my grandmother's hand. She died in 1978, and it was a jolt to see her familiar script after all these years, the delicate sweep and curve of her letters bearing on their backs the heavy legacy of Chocolate Chippy Cake, Jellied Salad Mould, Lazy Daisy Cake, and Peppermint Angel.

"Look!" I yelped. "Here's the recipe for Double Snackers!"

Double Snackers were Grandma's pièce de résistance: oatmeal coconut cookies with cream cheese chocolate filling. They were the Holy Grail of cookiedom. I would have stuck my tongue on a winter doorknob for the chance to eat a Double Snacker.

"Oh, yes," said my mother. "I was forever losing that recipe. I'd call your grandmother and ask her for it again and again. She must have copied it out a hundred times. I'm amazed I managed to hang onto that one."

While she flipped through the filing cards of her memory, quietly recollecting her daily phone conversations with her own mother (neither one risking the ruination of her clothes in dangerous weather), I jotted down the requirements and instructions for Double Snackers: Shape into balls the size of grapes . . . As I copied the recipe, I reflected on the links that were taking place through the act of writing: letter to letter, word to word, generation to generation, child to man. Oh, I couldn't wait to get home and whip up a batch! The lust was on me and there was only one way to satiate it.

Back in Vancouver, unpacked and eager to begin, I looked through my various papers. There was no Double Snackers recipe to be found. In a panic, I called my mother. "It must be here somewhere," she muttered. I could hear her flipping the pages of the church cookbooks. "I always did lose that recipe . . ."

Evidently, the tendency is genetic. So please—if anyone has the formula for Double Snackers, send it along. I need it in the worst possible way. We could do swapsies, even. How would you like Miss K. Halliday's Nice Drink for Hot Days? Summer is on the verge. It's just the thing for après croquet . . . And I guarantee—none of the ingredients will prove ruinous to either your health or your clothes.

Double Snackers

Preheat oven to 350°F.
Sift together:
>1 cup sifted all-purpose flour
>½ tsp. baking soda
>¼ tsp. salt

Set aside.
In another bowl, combine:
>½ cup shortening
>½ cup granulated sugar
>½ cup brown sugar, packed

Beat until light and creamy.
Blend in:
>1 egg
>½ tsp. vanilla

Stir in flour mixture. Add:
>1 cup cornflakes, crushed
>1 cup quick-cooking rolled oats
>½ cup dried coconut

Shape into balls the size of grapes. Place on greased cookie sheets and flatten with a fork. Bake for 8–10 minutes. Cool.

CHOCOLATE FILLING
Melt over hot water:
>6 oz. package semisweet chocolate chips
>1 Tbsp. water

Blend in:
>½ cup confectioner's sugar

Then blend in:
>3 oz. package soft cream cheese

Beat until smooth. Cool and spread between pairs of cookies as a filling.

interlocking pieces

This year, out of vocational necessity, I've spent a great deal of time in Winnipeg. My final sojourn there has just ended. It differed from the others in that I stayed with my parents rather than in a hotel. Though I hate to take issue with so celebrated an apothegmatist as Thomas Wolfe, I'm compelled to say that it's easy enough to go home again. The real problem arises when your mom and dad want to send half of home away with you, just as you're getting ready to leave.

"Will you go through some of these books and take away anything you'd like to have?" my father asked. What he had given me was an exercise in balancing sentiment with practicality. The volumes in question were old family heirlooms. Did I really want or need his boyhood *Book of Knowledge*, published in 1918, with its wonderfully informative entries on "The exciting game of stool ball" and "How to mark your name on fruit"? Or how about *My Bookhouse*, edited by Olive Beaupre Miller, which had been my mother's, and in whose six volumes I had pressed the leaves for a school project I never completed. Now those books exhale nostalgic, vegetative dust every time I open their pages.

More unsettling than their forgivable urge to disabuse themselves of these moldering souvenirs is the way they have started to apportion out more recently acquired goods and chattels. Intimations of mortality will do that to you. Any conversational gambit that spins on the admiration—genuine or contrived—of a teapot, clock, dresser, or end table engenders the response, "Fine. We'll put your name on it." And I have learned to be wary of cagey questions such as "How do you like these plates?"

The plates in question are not intended to harbour a dinner. Oh, no. Each one carries a warning that "faithful colour pigments may spoil food," for these plates are meant to festoon a wall. There's a whole series of butterflies, another of ducks on the wing, another of puppies with waterfowl in their jaws. Heaven knows, there's nothing wrong with them. But tastes vary, and the only way I would want them is if I took up skeet shooting. Conveying that information firmly but subtly is one of the challenges of my middle age.

"Perhaps you'd like some of the puzzles?" my mother asked. It was my last night home, and I was passing through the room in which she was working on a jigsaw picture of a country fair. Just over half of its 1,000 pieces had been conjoined, and you could see very clearly the stack of pumpkins and the rickety barn, and the beginnings of a square dance or similar hoe-down. This is one of several hundred jigsaw puzzles they've purchased or had given to them over time: diced-up reproductions of paintings by Great Masters, mountain landscapes, challenging abstracts.

"No thanks," I said, rather too quickly. "Uh—I just haven't got the mind for them," I added, by way of explanation.

"Hmmmmm," she said, turning the piece she held first one way, then another. "I don't blame you. They're addictive, and a terrible waste of time. And I always get to the end and find there's a piece missing. So I spend hours turning the house upside down and emptying the vacuum bag."

"Do you find it?"

"Sometimes yes, sometimes no. You just go on to the next. Ha! Got it!"

And she slipped the piece she had in hand into its rightful slot.

The next day I left and flew back to Vancouver, to the place that now comes most readily to mind when I pronounce that one weighty syllable: home. Whether this is through resolution and conviction or just pure dumb habit I am not equipped to say. The point is that flying west, with the weather clear and the crazy interlocking puzzle of the patchwork prairie rolling on and on 35,000 feet below, I understood that my mother had given me, by accident or design, all the reassurance I'll ever need in this ridiculous, exultant business of living. Piece by piece. Sometimes yes. Sometimes no. You just go on to the next.